a girl's Guide to College

Copyright © 2003, 2011 by Blue Mountain Arts, Inc.

Library of Congress Catalog Card Number: 2003010119
ISBN: 978-1-59842-597-0

▉ and Blue Mountain Press are registered in U.S. Patent and Trademark Office.
Certain trademarks are used under license.

Printed in China.
First printing of this edition: 2011

The Library of Congress has cataloged the first edition as follows:

Maynigo, Traci, 1981-
  a girl's guide to college : making the most of the best four years of your life /
Traci Maynigo.
     p. cm.
   ISBN 1-58786-012-0 (softcover : alk. paper)
  1. College student orientation—United States. 2. Women college students—United States—
Life skills guides. I. Title.

  LB2343.32.M325 2003
  378.1'982—dc21

                               2003010119
                                   CIP

Blue Mountain Arts, Inc.

P.O. Box 4549, Boulder, Colorado 80306

a girl's Guide to College

Making the most of the best four years of your life

Updated Edition

Traci Maynigo

Blue Mountain Press™

Boulder, Colorado

For my mom and dad, Tina and Ben...
I aspire to be like both of you every day.

Acknowledgments

Thank you, first and foremost, to my "college life consultants"—all extremely wise, open, and intelligent college girls from all over the country—whose personal stories and insights into college life not only helped make this updated edition accessible to a new generation, but also provided unique perspectives to complement my own. They are: Jennifer Conde, Macrina Cooper-White, Alisa delos Reyes, Diane Ferry, Kelly Flom, Courtney Grafton, Erica Irving, Valerie Leikina, Lizdibier Madera, Glorelys Mora-Liz, Hannah Rochau, Esme Rogers, Shanell Simmons, Carolyn Spalding, Sarah Szczepanski, Ashley Villanueva, Emily Fiona Weddle, Nicole White, and Serina Zorrilla. I'm so grateful to all of you for taking the time out of your summer to contribute to this book!

A huge thanks to Josh Lambert, who edited the first edition—and who is the best editor a first-time author could have asked for; as well as Patti Wayant and everyone at Blue Mountain Arts for their encouragement right from the beginning—starting with the original book and now this updated edition eight years later! A thank-you also goes to MaryEllen O'Brien for her editorial prowess—you truly have a way with words.

I am also grateful to my family for their undying love: my mom, Tina, and my sister, Tanya, without whose wisdom I wouldn't have survived college; my dad, Ben, for his fatherly advice and his expertise on all things legal and technological; and my pseudo-uncle, Daniel, and my brother, Raul, for their continued support.

A special thank-you to my pup, Bodie, who sat by my side throughout the entire writing process, keeping me motivated through every page and offering his doggie opinion as needed.

And finally, thank you to my best friend, roommate, and teammate, Jason Goss. You inspire me, you make me laugh, and I love you.

CONTENTS

Preface to the Updated Edition

When I wrote the first edition of *A Girl's Guide to College* as a senior in college in 2003, I didn't own a mobile phone (nor did most of my friends), and social-networking websites didn't exist. The idea of attending class "online" was a completely foreign concept, and for the most part, academic research required the Dewey decimal system and a long hunt through rows of dusty books in the physical space of a library. A great deal has changed in the past eight years. College social and academic life is dominated by technology, as students make weekend plans by checking their friends' social-networking profiles and fulfill course participation requirements by logging on to virtual learning environments.

This new edition has been updated to account for this major shift in the lifestyle of college students. While doing research for this update, however, I found that when it comes to college life, some things will forever remain the same. As such, much of the book's content remains unchanged from the original edition. After all, college life for any generation will invariably be a time of exploration and discovery, personal growth and its accompanying growing pains, and a setting for unparalleled and life-changing relationships and experiences.

Introduction: Well, it's about time, isn't it?

You've spent eighteen years prepping yourself for these next four years, and now that you're about to enter this other dimension, you're twitching with nervousness and excitement. You've probably heard it before: college isn't easy. In fact, it'll seem almost impossible at times. Of course, the last eighteen years probably weren't quite so easy either. It seems like just yesterday you were throwing animal crackers at your baby brother's face just to get your mom's attention. Soon after that, you were horrified at the sight of your school picture—your braces made your face look like the bumper of the family Volkswagen. Then it was the anguish of adolescence that tormented you—you were dismayed when you got your period, you wished your breasts would grow faster (or at least *evenly*), and you were confused at the funny feelings you were having over your first crush. Finally, high school came along and you hated the world and all its confining rules—you wished someone would at least *try* to understand you.

Yes, it's fair to say, you've been through a lot, and you're about to endure a whole lot more. College is tough, but in a different way. You'll get the independence you've been longing for, but you'll have to get used to all the responsibility it entails. Yet, as challenging as college is, it will also be four thrilling and unparalleled years that you'll want to relive forever after. It's the only time in your life when you'll be in a community with thousands of people just as young, confused, and energized as you. You'll learn from one another and share all sorts of experiences. And it's in this environment that you will discover yourself—who you are now and who you want to become. Plus, there are a million activities to sample, parties to go to, and people to meet (or date!)... who could forget all that?

With all this beautiful madness to participate in and self-discovery to do, why fret about less exciting stuff like getting through your classes, doing your laundry, and otherwise just learning to be a grownup? Well, it's because college just couldn't be college without the rest of it, too. And sometimes the best things in life come only with a little bit of suffering.

So, girls: get excited. You're going to love college.

CHAPTER ONE
THE SUMMER BEFORE COLLEGE: WHAT TO DO

Getting Ready: Bonding with Family and Friends

When the school year starts, you will enter an entirely new chapter of your life. In a way, it's like starting over completely—a rebirth. You're moving to a new place and an environment probably much different from your hometown or city. You will be among strangers at first, but soon many of them will form your new circle of friends and your family away from home. Not only will you need to learn to adjust to a new place and new people, but also to the very new stresses of college life. It's a juggling act. You're tossing up classes, activities, friends, work, and potentially a love life all at the same time. It's going to take a while to learn to manage them all without letting any one thing (or yourself, for that matter) fall to the floor. Sure, you may have juggled all these things in high school, but the stakes change once you are experiencing them in the college context. It may seem like it would be impossible to prepare yourself for all of this. And, for the most part, you can't. There are some things you can only learn from experience.

But knowing that you are about to cross a new threshold and change tremendously as a person, you can think of this summer as the last summer in which you can experience the best you that you are now. There's no telling what will happen next, so you might as well just relax, have fun, and go nuts. This is your last summer before college. It may be the last summer when no one expects anything from you. So live it up!

Do something new, different, crazy, stupid, or silly! Go on a road trip with your girlfriends. Have a sleepover for old time's sake. Skydive or bungee jump. Hit the hottest dance clubs downtown and dance till your feet hurt. Check out the hot surfers at the beach. Catch a rock concert. Go camping or fishing. Ride all the roller coasters at an amusement park. Travel!

> *"Relax!" That's what my friends kept telling me our last summer before college. I was anxiously making preparations for the upcoming year and had not taken the time to focus on just having fun and enjoying my last year of minimal responsibility. I gave in, ultimately, and my friends took me out one night. Unfortunately that night did not turn out as we expected. My friend's car broke down, and while waiting for her parents to rescue us, we sat in the car reminiscing about all the times we spent together. When I look back, I completely cherish that particular moment. We could have considered that night ruined, but instead, the unexpected nostalgic conversation gave us a chance to become aware of how many memories we all really shared and how close we had become throughout high school.*
>
> *— Jennifer Conde, University of South Florida*

Go crazy with your friends. Believe it or not, as the next four years go by—and as you and all your friends get in the habit of doing your own things during the summer—you may be seeing less and less of them. Take some risks this summer, and get your friends to join you. Don't paste yourself to the television screen and waste away these irreplaceable summer days. Do something different. Remember, these are the people you grew up with; they made you who you are. Show them love and make this last summer a memorable one. And while you're at it, take lots of pictures to hang up on your dorm-room wall as reminders of home.

If you've got some unresolved issues with any friends, now's the time to resolve them. Don't worry; your friends are probably just as ready as you are to patch things up. As you start this new experience and form new relationships, you want to feel secure about your relationships at home. Don't go off to college with emotional baggage (you'll already have enough boxes to carry). Wipe the slate clean.

> *I'd spent my high school summers at various camps and programs, and though these experiences had been invaluable, I knew exactly what I wanted to do the summer before college: absolutely nothing. My coastal town of Emerald Isle, NC, provided much needed rest and relaxation. I waited tables at a local restaurant, enjoyed dinners with my family, and lounged on the beach with my girlfriends daily. An impulsive road trip along the coast of California with my two best friends came in mid-July. For two weeks we trekked along the Pacific Coast Highway, crashing at friends' places in San Diego, Santa Barbara, and Los Angeles. We visited the Hollywood Walk of Fame, slept in a frat house in Isla Vista, shopped on Rodeo Drive (or rather, window-shopped), and ate at the famous In-N-Out Burger. I came to college that fall relaxed, revived, and appreciative of the time spent with my family and friends.*
>
> *— Courtney Grafton, Yale University*

Bond with your friends. You and your friends will be going through a lot of changes, so make the most of the time you have with them now. Finish up the end of the summer with a formal send-off party, making sure to invite everyone you want to see before you leave! Create a digital or hard-copy photo album of all your high school memories to share at the party, and make copies for everyone to take with them to college. As you say goodbye, remember that you aren't leaving forever—you'll be back during breaks!—and there are a million ways to stay in touch. Also, you may be surprised at how different friends deal with this transition out of high school and into college. Some can't wait to leave their old lives behind and start new ones, and some are not excited to do so. Be accepting of these different ways of coping with the change, and don't take it personally.

Plan to stay in touch with friends and family. Skype or video chat. Create a Facebook group. Promise to write on each of your friends' and relatives' Facebook walls at least once a semester. Create an e-mail thread to share news with friends and family. Call when you have time, and call back if the person was busy. Make plans during breaks. Text each other every couple of days. Visit each other's schools. Chat online. Remember to get in touch on birthdays.

> *I knew that when I got to college, I wasn't going to be speaking to my high school friends every day. And when I did speak to them, I sometimes found it difficult because they often didn't find my personal college experiences relatable to their own lives, and vice versa. My high school friends and I started a thread on Facebook where we would post funny stories or updates about our lives that we wanted to share with one another. It didn't take me long to realize that there's no need to get upset about drifting away from certain high school friends. I've grown apart from many people, not necessarily because of a dispute or irreconcilable differences, but simply because we have less in common now that we've adapted to our separate college environments.*
>
> *— Emily Fiona Weddle, University of Delaware*

Spend time with your family! As much as you'd like to deny it now, you will really miss them once you're at school. Homesickness will hit you over the head once in a while, and you may find yourself calling home more often than the obligatory weekly Sunday calls you initially agree to. So hit a movie with your little sister or brother, have a heart-to-heart with your mom, or organize a family barbecue. Often bonding time can be hidden in mundane tasks like grocery shopping or gardening. Your mom's nagging, your dad's corny jokes, and your brother's obnoxious armpit noises probably aren't so endearing to you now, but secretly you love them, and you'll love them even more when you're away from them. You'll be wishing you had spent more time with your family when you had the chance. Especially if you have a younger sibling, make time for him or her. Remember, you are the big sister and, therefore, a role model, a mentor, and a support system. Find a way to maintain that relationship when you're away.

Ways to bond with your family. Go to baseball and basketball games. Visit relatives that live near you. Go to the movies. Bring them college shopping. Go to the beach. Take a family road trip. Set aside nights to go out to dinner. Spend more time at home. Plan a board game night. Cook dinner together (you should learn a few recipes, anyway!). Play video games. Go hiking, bike riding, or camping. Spend time just talking and hanging out.

> *My sister was ten when I left for college. She was not looking forward to my leaving, and I was nervous about leaving her, too. I was worried that I wouldn't be there to teach her things I wished I'd learned from an older sister. I especially didn't want her to become as obsessed with weight as I am. Before I left, I sat her down and told her that as long as she focused on eating healthily (not dieting) and staying fit, she wouldn't have to worry about her weight. I emphasized that she should play the sports she loves in order to stay active. I'm really glad I had that talk with her, because now she plays varsity tennis as a seventh grader and is far more content with her body image than I even am with my own at this point!*
>
> *— Valerie Leikina, UMass Amherst*

If you are in a serious relationship, take some time to evaluate whether you should stay together. I know this advice seems harsh—and tough to follow—but many people later regret not doing this. In fact, I surveyed over one hundred college girls all across the U.S. and found that 1) more than 50 percent of them were in a serious relationship in high school; 2) almost 90 percent of those who were in relationships were no longer together with their significant others; and 3) almost 80 percent of them broke up just before, during, or immediately after their freshman year of college. Now every relationship is different and every situation is different, so your relationship may be one of the rare exceptions.

If you do plan on staying together and maintaining a long-distance relationship, prepare for a bumpy road ahead. Both of you will be going through a lot of changes, so expect and embrace change—in yourself and in your partner. Promise to always have open, honest conversations about your expectations and feelings as you go through these changes. And get comfortable with the possibility that as you both continue to change, you may not change and grow together—you may change and grow apart. Vow to each other that if either of you is living a less-than-fulfilling college life because of the strain of the relationship, you will break up. The most important thing is that both of you are able to maintain a balance between the relationship and college life; you should feel supported by your partner, but make an effort to meet new people, build a new life, and become an individual outside of your relationship. (For more on long-distance relationships, see Chapter 7.)

Breaking up is hard to do. It won't be easy no matter how you do it, but in fairness to both of you, do it in person, whether it's the summer before college or during a visit home on break. If circumstances make it impossible to meet face to face, talk on the phone or via Skype or video chat. Do not break up with your partner on his or her voice mail, by writing an e-mail, or through text message. These methods are cowardly and cruel. Breakups should happen face to face and in real time, so that both people can be upfront, sincere, and honest with each other in the moment.

If you have any doubts about whether you will be able to make the most of college while staying together, then you should break up and come to college unrestrained and unattached. Long-distance relationships can be unfulfilling and emotionally draining, especially when you are going through such a huge life transition. They can keep you from growing and thriving on your own.

Whatever decision you make about your relationship, remember it is your decision. No one else has the power to decide whether you and your partner should stay together. So be honest with yourself about what you want, and don't let anyone else pressure you into breaking up or staying together with your significant other. Make your decision based on what feels right to you—and have no regrets.

> *The guy I was dating in high school and the guy I broke up with my senior year of college were completely different people. And to be honest, I had changed, too. I realize now that in putting our relationship first, I missed out on so much of what college had to offer. I chose to apply only to colleges close to him, and I didn't participate in any sororities, clubs, or study abroad programs that I wanted to because I did not want to be away from him. There were friends I didn't make until much later in college and cute boys that I never talked to because I was so dedicated to him. More importantly, I missed out on the opportunity to take those four years and figure out who I was as an individual. By tying myself down, I grew up as part of a couple and not as my own person. Now that we are no longer together, it has been so exciting to discover more about myself and who I am—and it has been a huge confidence booster. I wish I had known back then how important it was to first become comfortable with who I am as an individual—separate from someone else.*
>
> *— Serina, George Mason University*

Get to know yourself—by yourself. Get to know who you are as someone separate from the people in your life, the high school you went to, your GPA, or your score on the SATs. Keep in mind: with all the changes that will be going on in your life in the next four years, the one thing that will always remain constant is yourself. It is you who will always be there, so value yourself. Give yourself some alone time, whether it's to go on a walk, write in a journal, or take a bubble bath—

whatever activity that allows you to become engrossed in you and only you. See what it's like to be without other people. This time for yourself won't necessarily reveal to you anything spectacular about your purpose in life, but it isn't meant to. You'll have lots of time in college (and the rest of your life, for that matter) to discover who you are. Just use this time to appreciate who you are now, regardless of the people or things surrounding you. Take some time to think about what you are interested in, what makes you happy, what you are passionate about.

Write down your goals. They can be goals for your first year of college, goals for when you're finished with college, or even goals for ten years from now. Get a sense of what direction you're headed, so you can begin to create a path—step by step.

Get a summer job and SAVE MONEY. You'll need it, trust me. You should definitely work during the school year (if not to go toward tuition, then for spending money), but it's not something you'll want to think about immediately when you're trying to get settled. If you don't have much work experience already, consider a job that is related to your long-term career interests or that will teach you skills necessary for getting a job in college. Otherwise, get a job that involves minimal stress and flexible hours. Whatever you do, make sure you leave yourself some time to hang out with friends and family and prepare for school.

Great summer jobs: Try waiting tables or being a hostess at a restaurant or for a caterer (free food!). Work at a clothing store (discounts!). Work for a temp agency as a secretary, administrative assistant, or receptionist. Housesit, pet-sit, or babysit. Deliver pizza. Scoop ice cream. Be a lifeguard. Work as a barista at a café or coffee shop. Work with children at a church, daycare, or summer camp. Work at your local health club or gym.

Learn about your school. Find out what it has to offer. If you have the time and it's not too far, consider going to your school for a visit. Otherwise, check out its website. For more insider information from students, check blogs and websites like Talk.CollegeConfidential.com and CollegeView.com. Don't just find out about classes, but also about options for extracurricular activities and about the surrounding area. Talk to current students. If you know someone who either goes there or graduated recently, give him or her a call. Ask that person questions that the website and campus tour guide won't be able to answer, like where you should hang out and what dining hall entrees to avoid. Don't forget to also join the Facebook groups for your school and your incoming class.

If your college has any kind of preorientation program, sign yourself up! Many colleges offer programs for incoming freshman during the summer—usually during the two or three weeks before classes start. They could involve anything from camping to community service—all with the purpose of allowing you to bond with your future classmates. Get a head start on making friends, and join in!

Getting to know your new home a little bit beforehand will pay off when you get there. You'll be able to spend more time meeting new people while most of your classmates are frantically trying to find their way to the dining hall. That said, don't stress too much about your preliminary fact-finding because your expectations and plans will be eradicated soon after you get to school. Just get a general idea, and then leave the rest to discover when you get there. It's more fun that way, anyway. And above all, get excited! As overwhelming as this transition seems, you are in for an unforgettable experience.

———

In a survey, I asked over a hundred current college girls, "What is the one thing you wish you had known before you went off to college?" Here are the ten most popular answers:

1. That Greek life was such a big deal on campus—and that it is such a big party school!
2. That going to a small school would make it feel like high school all over again.
3. That joining clubs and organizations is the best way to meet people.
4. That classes are much harder than they were in high school!
5. That when making friends, it helps to be outgoing—and it isn't as easy as it was in kindergarten!

6. That you don't need to take everything so seriously—enjoy it!
7. That there are mental-health services available.
8. That the professor-student relationship is really important.
9. That the dining hall food was so bad.
10. That at a big school, it's easy to feel like you get lost in the crowd.

Packing Up:
Getting There with What You Need

All right, girls, the end of the summer is near, and as much as you would love to keep putting it off, it's time to start packing. Unfortunately, it's just not physically possible to transport everything in your room at home directly to your dorm room in one fell swoop, sans-boxes, sans-mess, sans-hassle. But (sigh) as I mentioned earlier, the best things only come with just a little bit of suffering. I like to think of packing as an opportunity to refurbish my wardrobe. As I carefully select what to pack and what not to pack, I realize that with every article I leave behind, I'm opening up a door for a new one later on. And I do love to buy new clothes.

Be a minimalist—only bring what you know you will use. This is your chance to rummage through your closet and get rid of every skirt, top, and pair of jeans that you thought you would wear again but never have. Consider taking them to a thrift shop or giving them to a friend or relative who might actually wear them.

What you bring also depends on how far away from home you are going. If you are going far enough to have to hop on a plane to get there, you can just pack as much as the airline weight limit allows (or as much as you can carry on your own!). As for everything else, you can either mail a few boxes to your dorm or buy whatever you need when you get to school. Can't decide what to bring, what to mail, and what to buy? Bring with you everything you know you will need immediately (clothes for the current season, toiletries, personal items); ship nonseasonal clothes; and buy items for your dorm room (appliances, space-savers, snacks) when you get there.

Pack clothes according to when you will be returning home for break. If you know you will be going home for fall break (usually Thanksgiving), bring only fall clothes with you. Then when you return from fall break, you can bring your winter clothes back with you. When you return home for winter break, bring spring clothes with you. You get the idea.

If you are mailing packages to your dorm, make sure to find out about the mail delivery system at your school. At some schools, you have your own PO box where you can't receive big boxes, so you have to have packages delivered elsewhere—to your dorm address or a specific building—depending on whether you are using USPS, FedEx, or UPS. Also, keep in mind that the mail and delivery systems at colleges can be very slow, so if you are expecting something, be patient, and keep checking in with whoever receives packages! Sometimes nagging helps.

Check out your dorm room ahead of time, if you can. Some colleges have virtual tours on their websites, or if you live close enough, consider going for a visit. Knowing how much space you have will aid in the packing process. If you are unable to check out your dorm, make two packing lists: must-haves and might-haves. Only pack the must-haves, and mail or buy the might-haves when you get there.

Remember where you're going and what the weather is like. The weather may be frigid or it may be sweltering, or it may be somewhere in between. Pack accordingly.

Cut down on clothes that require too much maintenance. You will need a formal dress or two and a couple of business-casual outfits, but other than that, do yourself a favor and don't bring clothes that are hard to take care of. This includes clothes that require dry cleaning, hand washing, and ironing. Given the rapid pace of your college life, you will not want to take much time for these tedious tasks.

Just keep it simple. Less really is more in this case, because who knows how much space you'll have in your dorm room. Plus, you'll be moving so often (at least twice a year—once in September and again in

May!) that you'll be grateful to have fewer boxes to lug. You may be tempted to bring *everything*. Trust me, you won't even use half of it. Only bring the essentials.

Feel free to reinvent your wardrobe, but don't stray too far from what you're comfortable wearing. After all, you want your classmates to get to know the authentic you, even if it is the authentic you with a little bit of added panache. You may be having flashbacks to the first day of school every September in your middle or high school years (not too long ago, though it may seem so) when you spent two hours trying on outfits the night before. You wanted to wear something new and different so somehow you would seem like a new and different person to these kids who had known you since you were eating glue and crayons. Well, this time around, you'll be new and different to everyone you meet, no matter what you're wearing, so don't worry too much about it.

Consider not buying any new clothes until you get to school and can get a sense of the style climate. Then you can decide if you want to sport the standard look or veer away from the norm. If comfort is your priority, bring what you need and buy what you're comfortable wearing. If standing out among your peers is your main concern, check out the current trends when you get there so you can eventually turn some heads and start some trends of your own. The style climate, however, shouldn't dictate your own personal style, but it can help with the editing process. What matters is that you feel good in your clothes.

Let's get packing! I've given you some basic pointers for packing strategies, but ultimately it comes down to you and what you know you need. Now, I know packing can be overwhelming, so I'm not going to leave you on your own just yet! Following is an ultimate college packing list—along with explanations for some of the essential items—that you can use as a guide as you pack and shop for college. Keep in mind that this list is *only a guide.* You absolutely should not pack everything—only what you are pretty sure you already have or will need.

A GIRL'S GUIDE TO COLLEGE
ULTIMATE COLLEGE PACKING LIST

CLOTHING

☐ **Underwear (bras and panties) and socks.** Pack them all! Buy underwear and socks in bulk, and shove them into every crevice of your suitcase. You'll soon find that as laundry becomes the last thing on your priority list (particularly during paper-writing stress or exam time), you'll appreciate the fact that you're wearing clean underwear and socks under your dirty clothes.

☐ **Thermal underwear or long johns (one set).** If you are going to school where it gets extremely cold in the wintertime—cold enough that a winter coat isn't enough—these will come in handy.

☐ **Sweatpants, sweatshirts/fleeces/hoodies, T-shirts/tanks.** Comfort is key, so bring a bunch of these. You can also stock up on your school's paraphernalia once you get there and show your school spirit!

☐ **Jeans.** Bring a few good pairs.

☐ **Pajamas (a few sets) and a big, comfy bathrobe and slippers.** You can wear your bathrobe lounging in your room, to and from the bathroom, or to keep toasty warm when your heater breaks down.

☐ **Cocktail dresses and formal dresses (two or three).** Bring your prom dress if you'd wear it again. You will most likely have opportunities to attend formals or semiformals, whether they are fraternity or sorority formals or school-sponsored balls or dances.

☐ **Going-out/party outfits.** You'll want several of these.

☐ **Business-casual outfits (two).** You never know when you'll have to attend an event that requires you to dress professionally, and you will also be attending internship and job interviews.

☐ **Theme outfits, costumes, crazy shirts/hats/shoes/accessories.** You will have the option of attending various theme parties for which you will want to sport the right outfit. Bring anything that you think could come in handy (Hawaiian lei for a luau, bell-bottoms for the '60s, off-the-shoulder shirt and spandex for the '80s). If you don't have anything theme oriented, don't worry—it will be fun to shop with friends when the need arises.

☐ **Workout clothes.** Don't forget sports bras.

☐ **Swimsuits.** Swimming makes for a relaxing and fun workout, and if you are going to school by the beach, you want to be well-equipped for bumming on the shore. Bring at least two: one for recreation and relaxation, and one for exercise.

☐ **Accessories.** These include belts (one or two); a small purse, handbag, or wristlet to carry your cell, cash, and ID when you go out; your favorite jewelry; and a pair of sunglasses. But only bring your favorites, because you won't use everything

☐ **Footwear.** Shoes take up space and they are heavy, so only bring one pair of each kind: slippers, sneakers, sandals, rain/snow boots, leather boots, heels, and flats. As for flip-flops, you might bring two pairs of those— one to wear in the shower, for sure, and another to conveniently slip on when the weather is warm and you are in a rush to get somewhere (like a 9:00 a.m. class that you are constantly late for).

☐ **Outerwear.** Depending on where you're going, you'll have to be prepared for inclement weather, so be sure to bring a raincoat and a jacket or windbreaker. Bring a few umbrellas, because they are easy to lose! Bring one really big one for those heavy rains and a couple pocket-sized ones that you can carry around in case of emergency. If you're going someplace cold, you'll need a winter coat or parka, warm gloves, a winter scarf, and a winter hat and/or earmuffs.

TOILETRIES AND FIRST AID/ILLNESS

Bring only what you know you will use. For items that you normally go through quickly and in large amounts, like dental floss or soap, you might consider buying a bunch at home and storing them in a closet or under your bed at school. This will decrease the number of trips you have to make to the store when you are busy with college life.

☐ **Shower caddy/basket/bucket and makeup/toiletries bag.** Use these to transport your toiletries between your room and the bathroom.

☐ **Towels.** Bring a ton of them in various sizes (face, hand, and bath). Consider buying ones that are easy to recognize (maybe in bright colors or patterns), or at least put your name on them.

☐ **Skin care.** Face wash, exfoliant, face mask, toner, moisturizer, lip balm, sunscreen for face, tweezers, cotton balls, tissues, and makeup.

☐ **Body care.** Soap, shower gel, or body wash; plastic, covered soap dish (if you use soap); loofah (if you use shower gel or body wash); deodorant or antiperspirant; lotion; sunscreen; perfume; tampons and/or pads; razor and shaving cream/gel (or waxing kit).

☐ **Manicure/pedicure.** Nail clipper, nail file, nail polish, nail polish remover.

☐ **Hair care.** Shampoo, conditioner, hairbrush and/or comb, hair dryer, flat iron and/or curling iron, styling products, and hair accessories.

☐ **Dental care.** Toothbrush and toothpaste, small cup (for gargling), floss, and mouthwash.

☐ **Vitamins and medicine.** It's easy to get sick in college because of lack of sleep, high stress, and frequent interaction with classmates. Take your vitamins regularly, use hand sanitizer, and stock up on any medicine you might need, so you won't have to run to the drugstore late at night when you are hacking up a lung while studying for a final exam.

First-aid kit musts:

☐ Antibiotic ointment and hydrogen peroxide/rubbing alcohol)
☐ Vitamin supplements (especially multivitamin, calcium, and vitamin D)
☐ Cold medicine
☐ Antacid
☐ Adhesive bandages
☐ Cough drops
☐ PMS medication
☐ Cold prevention
☐ Pain reliever (such as aspirin or ibuprofen)

BEDDING

☐ **Sheets and pillowcases.** Dorm rooms have extra-long beds, so you'll need extra-long sheets. Bring at least two sets of sheets and pillowcases, so you'll have backups for when you don't have time to do laundry.

☐ **Duvet, duvet cover, and pillows.** Bring the ones from your bed at home. If you've got a body pillow or memory foam pillow at home, bring that, too! Anything you can do to make your bed comfy.

☐ **Extra blankets and/or quilts.**

☐ **Egg crate or traditional mattress pad or bed topper.** Dorm room beds are not very comfortable. One of these will help make your bed feel more like the one you sleep on at home.

LAUNDRY

☐ **Laundry bag and/or basket.** The best kind serves as both a hamper and a bag for transporting your laundry. Consider getting one that has dividers to make sorting easier.

☐ **Drying rack.** You'll need this for your bras and other delicate clothing that can't be put in the dryer—or for when you don't have time to throw your laundry load in the dryer!

☐ **Quarters.** At most colleges, in order to use a washer or dryer you just swipe a prepaid laundry card, but some schools do still use the older machines that require quarters. Find out if your school has the old ones, and if so, bring rolls of quarters!

☐ **Laundry detergent, fabric softener, bleach, and stain lifter.** Buy in bulk whenever you can.

SCHOOL STUFF

You can always buy school supplies when you get to school, but don't just go to the school's bookstore, which will charge you three times as much as one of the big-box stores. However, if you happen to have some supplies at home or have room in your suitcase to buy them ahead of time, go for it!

☐ **Backpack/messenger bag.** You'll need something to carry your heavy textbooks in. Make sure it's sturdy and spacious and has room for your laptop if you plan on using one.

☐ **Academic planner/calendar.** You'll need to keep track of your classes, assignments, and schedule, so make sure you have something to keep you organized. If you have a calendar application on your laptop or mobile device, use that; otherwise, buy a planner with a calendar in it. They come in various types and sizes, so pick one that suits your lifestyle.

☐ **Old essays from high school.** Believe it or not, you might read some of the same literature or be assigned some similar topics. Bring some of your best essays from high school, as they could make a good reference.

☐ **Grammar and style guides.** The most common ones used in college are the *MLA Handbook for Writers of Research Papers* and *The Elements of Style*. Others include *The Chicago Manual of Style* (for book publishing),

The Associated Press Stylebook (for journalism), and *Publication Manual of the American Psychological Association* (for social sciences).

☐ **Dictionary and thesaurus.** You'll want these if for some reason you can't look things up online.

☐ **Miscellaneous supplies.**

☐ Binder(s)
☐ Folders
☐ Pencils
☐ Permanent markers
☐ Stapler and staples
☐ Scissors
☐ Thumbtacks or pushpins
☐ Index cards
☐ Correction fluid, tapes, or pens
☐ Printer paper
☐ Stamps
☐ Wrapping paper and ribbon or gift bags

☐ Notebooks and/or notepads
☐ Pens
☐ Pencil sharpener
☐ Highlighters
☐ Tape
☐ Paper clips
☐ Rubber bands
☐ Glue stick or rubber cement
☐ Sticky notes
☐ Envelopes
☐ Stationery

TECHNOLOGY

☐ **Laptop (with case or bag) or desktop computer.** If you've already got a computer, bring it! If not, and you can afford to buy one, consider getting a laptop for its portability. Check your school's store for discounts on hardware and software—chances are, you can get at least 10 percent off! If you don't have or can't afford a computer, don't worry—your school probably has a computer lab available for student use.

☐ **Webcam.** Many laptops have webcams built in, and it's great to have one so you can video chat or Skype with friends and family.

☐ **E-book reader.** If you've already got one, definitely bring it, or consider buying one if you can afford it. At many schools you can buy your textbooks in e-book format, or many of your readings will be provided as PDFs that you can view on an e-reader. Using an electronic reading device for as many of your readings as possible will not only save you money, but also save you from back and shoulder pain (fewer heavy textbooks!).

☐ **Printer.** You don't have to have your own printer, as most colleges have computer labs with printers. However, if you have one or can afford to buy one, bring it. You never know when you'll need to print something—it could be when the computer labs are closed. And don't forget to bring extra ink!

☐ **USB flash/thumb drive and hard drive.** A thumb drive is a must! You'll need to be able to transport your electronic files easily. An additional hard drive is also a good idea for backing up all your documents in case your computer crashes.

☐ **Computer software and electronic equipment.** These include computer cables, extension cords, power strips, adapters, a backup hard drive, and chargers for your cell phone, iPod, camera, etc.

☐ **Entertainment.** A cell phone, television, digital camera, headphones, DVD player, iPod/MP3 player and speakers.

RECREATION

Make sure you bring supplies and equipment for your hobbies and recreational activities. It's important to make time for nonschool-related things—to keep yourself balanced and refreshed. Don't worry if you don't have room for or don't own any equipment, as you may be able to rent it from your school gym.

☐ Athletic equipment (rollerblades, roller skates, skateboard, scooter, bicycle, etc.; yoga mat; free weights; basketball; football; etc.), along with security and safety gear (lock and chain, helmet, knee and elbow pads)
☐ Board games
☐ Sleeping bag
☐ Deck of cards
☐ Books (for pleasure reading)
☐ Your favorite DVDs
☐ Music (MP3s, CDs, etc.)
☐ Journal
☐ Art and/or hobby supplies

MISCELLANEOUS

☐ **Earplugs and eye mask.** For when your roommate is up late and you need to get your sleep.

☐ **Durable water bottle and portable mug.** You should be bringing water with you wherever you go, and you can fill the portable mug with coffee or tea from the dining hall.

☐ **Something meaningful from home.** Think of this as your transitional object or security blanket. Whether it's a favorite stuffed animal, a throw pillow, or a knickknack, bring it with you to remind you of home.

☐ **Padlock.** You'll need this for your hall locker, if your school has these, or for your gym locker if you use the gym.

☐ **Household items.** Consider bringing things like duct tape and/or packing tape, a pocketknife, safety pins, a sewing kit, superglue, batteries, light bulbs, a tool kit, and a flashlight.

DORM

Some of this stuff you should definitely buy, some you won't know if you have space for until you see how big your dorm room is, and some you and your roommate should divvy up—you won't need two microwaves! For more tips on shopping for and decorating your dorm room, see Chapter 2. In the meantime, here are a few things to note about some of these items.

☐ **Furniture and accessories.** You will probably have to see your dorm room first before you consider these items: floor lamp and/or hanging lamp, bookshelf, full-length mirror, ottoman (with storage), rug, a comfortable chair, like a beanbag chair, and a love seat.

☐ **Desk supplies.** Assuming a desk is provided, you'll need a desk lamp and/or bedside lamp, drawer organizers, and a wastebasket.

☐ **Any kind of space-savers.** Plastic drawer units, storage bins, etc.

☐ **Wall decor.** Besides photographs, posters, tapestries, and magazine clippings, you might also want to have a bulletin board and a dry-erase board and markers.

☐ **Hangers (the space-saving kind).** Don't forget to include the kinds meant for hanging pants and skirts and padded ones to prevent shoulder nubbies in knit tops.

☐ **Alarm clock.** Can't be late for class!

☐ **Small fan and/or white noise machine.** The fan can double as an AC substitute (if your school doesn't have AC) and also as a white noise machine to help lull you to sleep. Sometimes dorm buildings are so loud that it helps to have something to drown out the noise.

☐ **Small space heater.** You never know how temperamental your dorm's heat could be, or maybe you just like to keep extra toasty warm.

☐ **Plastic hooks.** These usually have adhesive on the back of them so you can put them anywhere. You can use them to hang your jacket, your towels, your keys, whatever.

☐ **Adhesive wall putty/strips.** You'll need these to hang up your posters and photographs—it's easier on the wall paint, so you don't have to worry about peeling.

☐ **Hanging shoe rack.** This usually goes behind a door, and it's a space-saving way to store shoes.

☐ **Iron and ironing board or handheld steamer.** You should check with your roommate first to coordinate bringing these items.

CULINARY

If you plan on using your dorm room as your own little kitchen, you will probably need most of these supplies. Otherwise, you may not need any of it. Be sure to check your school's policy on appliances, like microwaves and mini-fridges, to make sure you are allowed to have them—some have an "If it glows, it goes!" policy. Be sure to coordinate with your roommate.

☐ Microwave and mini-fridge (if allowed) OR a micro fridge (a combination of both)
☐ Utensils
☐ Bottle opener
☐ Can opener
☐ Plastic wrap and aluminum foil
☐ Snacks and staples (tea bags, coffee, granola bars, cereal, soup, trail mix, etc.)
☐ Toaster or toaster oven (if allowed)
☐ Coffeemaker (if allowed)
☐ Water filter
☐ Plastic storage containers
☐ Corkscrew
☐ Plastic storage bags (various sizes)
☐ Durable and microwavable plates, bowls, cups, and mugs

CLEANING

You'll want to coordinate with your roommate on these items, too.

☐ Broom and dustpan
☐ Sponges
☐ Trash bags
☐ All-purpose cleaner
☐ Odor eliminator
☐ Dishwashing liquid
☐ Portable vacuum
☐ Paper towels
☐ Cleaning wipes
☐ Lint roller

CHAPTER TWO

YOUR NEW HOME: TURNING A SHOEBOX INTO A PALACE

You're standing in the hallway next to all your boxes piled two feet over your head, and you look inside your dorm room and wonder, "How am I going to fit all of *this* into *that?*" It looks about as easy as fitting into a pair of jeans from fifth grade. Well, it can be done. With luck, you didn't pack more than the necessities in the first place (see Chapter 1), but if you did, you can always send the surplus home. Not only do you have to worry about fitting everything into your room, but also about turning it into your ideal bedroom, living room, office, and kitchen at the same time. You've got to transform this little shoebox into your very own palace.

My jaw dropped when I unlocked my room for the first time and I saw how small, dim, and plain the space looked. There were only two beds, two dressers, two desks, and two closets. When the sun went down, the room was pitch black. There was no way I was going to live in this room as it was. Something had to be done. I went shopping for bed risers, room lamps, colorful bed sets, and wallpaper to decorate my wall with pictures of friends and family. Later on in the semester, my roommate and I decorated the windows with different school stickers and painted them with window paint markers. We also rearranged our beds and desks to make the room way more spacious, lively, and homey than it was originally. It made such a big difference!

— Shanell Simmons, Temple University

As I mentioned in the previous chapter, it would be a good idea to check out your dorm room (or any dorm room in your building) before you pack and move (and shop!)—not only to see how much space you have, but also what kind of furniture is already provided. Chances are, your dorm room will come with a bed, desk, desk chair, closet, and dresser—and possibly a bookshelf and/or wall mirror. So if any of these items are on your shopping or packing list, you can probably cross them off. Additionally, if your room is in a suite, you may also have a living room and/or a kitchen to furnish—with the help of your suitemates, of course!

Remember you will have a roommate with whom you will be sharing your space. Consult her before you paint a life-size self-portrait on the ceiling or construct your own replica of the Empire State Building in the center of the room. Compromise with her, but also find some space that you can make your own.

Once you've carved out your own space, make it comfortable and make it yours, because it is *your* space. Design your environment to reflect your ideal state of consciousness. Everything you own is alive with energy. You receive impressions from the possessions that surround you that enhance or detract from your life experience. If something you have brings back bad memories or associations, get rid of it. If it makes you feel good, keep it.

Modify your space to fit your lifestyle. Because of the nature of college life, your dorm room may exist for you as more than just a bedroom. It may not only be where you sleep, but also where you study, where you cook and eat, where you entertain guests, where you relax by yourself, and where you veg in front of the television. Although space may make it difficult, do your best to carve out separate spaces for each activity. Consider the main functions of your dorm room and equip, arrange, and decorate to suit each function.

▷ **Bedroom:** Your dorm will definitely be where you sleep, so make your bed comfortable and relaxing, whether it's by using a mattress pad; bringing a few extra pillows and blankets, a duvet, or a body pillow from home; or even having your favorite stuffed animal. Bring with you other elements that help you sleep, whether it's a white noise machine (or a small fan works, too), a nightlight, or a reliable and not-too-jarring alarm clock.

Functionality is everything. Your dorm should be arranged so that everything is where it is most convenient for your lifestyle. Find permanent homes for your keys, cell phone, umbrellas, and wallet.

▷ **Office:** If you plan on studying in your dorm room, your desk space should be well organized and spacious, with all supplies, hardware, and books in their own accessible places. You should have a bright incandescent or halogen desk lamp to help you stay focused and alert while you work. Also, your desk chair should be comfortable; if the one they provide for you isn't ideal, at least add a cushion to the seat. Although it may be tempting to study on your bed, resist! While you're reading your psychology textbook, you might be too tempted to rest your head for a minute—which then turns into an hour-long nap!

▷ **Kitchen:** If you plan on doing some cooking and/or eating in your dorm room, you will need to equip yourself with the necessary appliances—especially a mini-fridge and microwave, if they are allowed, as well as some storage space for your cookware, dishware, and utensils.

▷ **Living room:** The priority in a living room is enough seating, especially if you plan on entertaining guests. Whether you have a few beanbag chairs, an ottoman (with storage in it!), a papasan chair, a bunch of gigantic pillows, or even a loveseat or futon—whatever fits!—offer your guests a few seating options. Consider creating a little entertainment area, perhaps with a TV (or your laptop), a set of speakers, and an iPod dock.

If it's going to be in your room, it should serve an important function, carry a special memory, or have been created by you or someone you care about.

Make storage and organization a priority. Your dorm room may be small, but you're not the only one with this problem! Pretty much every freshman's first dorm room is the size of a shoebox. You will survive, I promise, as long as you make the most of your space. The best way to do this is to create as much storage as possible. Consider lofting your bed, if lofts are permitted at your school and you wouldn't mind climbing up into your bed every night. If they aren't allowed, elevate your bed with cinderblocks, which are cheap and available at any hardware store. Utilize the space under your bed to store off-season clothing in big plastic bins. Hide your new storage space by using fabric or another sheet as a bed skirt. Organize all your school supplies and jewelry in drawer units, arrange your shoes in an over-the-door shoe rack, and store your scarves and hats in hanging fabric shelves in your closet.

> *The quest to make my room college friendly was not as difficult as I thought it would be. My mission was to create a room that would have as much hidden storage as possible and that could also double as an escape from the hectic life of a college student. I bought three storage bins that were around ten dollars each and tucked them under my bed. I also bought an ottoman that gave me extra seating when I needed it and also doubled as an extra place for storage. Lastly, I went with the motto "Less is more." I tried to keep things as simple as could be.*
>
> *— Jennifer Conde, University of South Florida*

Shopping for your dorm. When shopping for dorm room furniture, think cheap. You'll only be living in this room for a year. If you buy cheap furniture, you can sell it at the end of the spring semester, so you won't have to worry about storing it. If you want your room to be more unique, cozy, and homey, shop at thrift stores, garage sales, moving sales, or auctions, or buy used furniture from family or friends. Or if you like the modern look of some of the new dorm furniture and want to buy new, aim for quality—after all, if you are going to buy new, you might as well aim to use the same dorm wares throughout your four years in college. And by the way, if you are sharing shopping expenses with a roommate or suitemates, make sure to keep track of who is buying what so you know who brings each item home at the end of the year.

The wall is your canvas—use it to reflect your passions. Chances are, you won't have that much room in your dorm to spice things up with more furniture—but you will definitely have some blank walls to work with! When it comes to wall decor, be thoughtful and selective, because what goes on your walls will reflect your personality. Remember, you're not just trying to cover wall space, you're also trying to show people who you are. Do you like to travel? Put up maps of the places you have visited or that you plan on visiting. Are you a musician? Display sheet music or hang up your instruments. Hang any objects that interest you, like a bowler hat or a trumpet or whatever is taking up space in your closet. Bulletin or corkboards are great for the wall because they leave you space and freedom to experiment, plus they are also functional. Whatever you decide to put on your wall, keep in mind that you will have to remove everything at the end of the year. Be careful with sticky tape, as it will peel paint from your walls and your school will make you pay for the damage. Use adhesive putty instead, or consider framing and hanging photos instead of taping them to your wall—it looks classier and minimizes the time it will take to remove them from the wall at the end of the year.

Wall decor ideas: Your favorite photos in a collage frame. Wall sticker decals. Mural of magazine covers. Funny lists. Hanging tapestries. Your own artwork. Your friends' artwork. Cards and postcards from family and friends. Prints of your favorite paintings. Fun T-shirts. Paint by number pictures. Mirrors. Empty picture frames. Shelves hung vertically. Album covers. Black-and-white photos of your hometown. Photos hung on a clothesline stretching across a wall.

Put up lots of photos. These can be pictures of your family and friends at home or photographs of your crazy times at school as the year progresses. You can either put them up as is or frame them first. Be creative with your photographs. Make collages, frame your mirror or windows with them, or tape them to the front of your door to show your visitors how social you are.

Posters are a great way to fill up space and show your interests, but refrain from shopping for them at your school's bookstore, unless you want to have the same posters as everyone else in your school. Shop online for posters that suit your personality. Consider also getting posters that will be useful to you as a college student: the periodic table, a world map, the different parts of the brain, grammar rules—you get the idea.

Don't forget about the floor, windows, and ceiling! Area rugs with great patterns, or oddly shaped fuzzy ones, can easily command a room. Hang a patterned curtain on your window, place cushions on a window seat if you have one, or decorate the window pane with gel gems, decals, or washable paint. Hang a lamp or a mobile from your ceiling.

Lighting. It's easy to forget about the importance of lighting. It can have a significant effect on the ambience of your dorm room, and it's a simple and cost-effective way of taking control of the atmosphere. Soft lighting is more relaxing, intimate, and stress-free. Bright lighting implies work, concentration, and intellectual stimulation but can sometimes result in stress. Make a harsh light warmer by angling it toward the wall or upward into a corner.

> For me, lighting is the most crucial part of getting my dorm room to feel like home. The fluorescent lights in the dorms were cold and unfriendly, so I bought a floor lamp with moveable lights on it so I could adjust the lighting to make the room feel more warm and inviting. It makes such a big difference!
>
> — Carolyn Spalding, Lafayette College

There are five kinds of lighting: fluorescent, halogen, incandescent, natural (sunlight), and fire (candles). Avoid fluorescent light, as it is unsettling and even irritating. Generally, halogen is good for anything needing precision and fine concentration, but a bright incandescent light works just as well. Incandescent light is good for creating a warm and comforting atmosphere, especially in the wintertime. Natural light is the best kind of lighting and should be used whenever possible, especially for reading in the morning. If allowed, candles are great for relaxation.

Put up holiday lights! Not only are they inexpensive, but they can also do wonders for the ambience. Depending on the colors you use and how many you put up, you can create an atmosphere that's romantic or an environment fit for partying. They also make great nightlights.

Pick a color scheme. Choose two or three different colors that complement each other and try to coordinate the things in your room with those colors. Determine your color scheme by picking the most noticeable colors from one of your favorite wall hangings or one major piece of furniture. Keep in mind that particular colors can also say something about your personality, and they have an effect on the feelings you and your guests have when inside your room. Warm colors (red, orange, yellow) denote energy, drama, and passion. Cool colors (blue, green, charcoal, light neutrals) denote calm and relaxation.

I didn't know what my dorm room was going to look like before I moved in. All I knew was that I would be staying in a single, which meant I didn't have a roommate. It turned out that I would have one of the larger rooms on the floor because it was a corner room. More space meant that people would migrate to my room to hang out. The only problem was that I didn't have any furniture, aside from what was in the room when I moved in: a bed, a desk, a dresser, and a chair. I had to get creative. Everything became a chair. Pillows on top of my mini-fridge and storage bins made them into seats. The windowsill made a perfect bench for two. You just have to take what you have and make the best of it!

— Esme Rogers, Howard University

Don't underestimate the value of plants and flowers (even fake ones). They can really add life to a room, even if they aren't alive. If you can handle the responsibility of watering on a regular basis, buy a nice, big, potted plant and situate it in the corner of the room. Even a small one is okay, as long as you put it somewhere visible. Just don't forget to take care of it. And buy something rugged enough to survive without water during your vacations. Now if the responsibility of another life is too much for you to handle—heck, you forget to feed *yourself* sometimes—then buy a fake plant or a vase with fake or real flowers. With real flowers, all you have to do is let them sit there until they start to smell bad (which means they are dying), then buy a new bouquet. Fake or dried ones can sit there forever.

Making a small space look big. Use lots of mirrors, lamps, and uplights. Keep the scheme monochromatic (the simpler the design, the bigger the space will feel). Use several different forms of lighting to create the illusion of a more complex space. Focus the lighting on the opposite side of the room to make it look longer. Cover your windows with light-colored curtains that are wider than the window but not see-through. Use minimal furnishings and accessories. Keep the bed and seating low. Make sure wall coverings and fabric patterns are small and widely spaced. Cool colors on walls make a room feel cooler and bigger by making the walls recede visually, so choose cool colors when picking your wall decor.

CHAPTER THREE

FRIEND OR ENEMY: GETTING ALONG WITH YOUR ROOMMATE

Not only does your dorm room come with a bed and a desk, but also in all likelihood with a real live person. Unfortunately, much to your chagrin, this real live person won't be as willing to serve you as your coffee table or towel rack. If you've shared a room with someone before, you know how difficult it can be to define each other's space and respect each other's privacy. And in college, it won't be like sharing a room with your little sister. You won't be able to call on Mom or Dad to solve disputes. Your roommate will be at first a stranger, and depending on how you get along, she may just be your roommate (nothing more, nothing less) or she may become your best friend or your biggest enemy.

My sophomore-year roommate seemed like a perfectly nice girl. Excited, I told her that she could borrow my clothes, use my makeup, and have any of the food in the fridge. Soon cities of crumbs emerged on my futon, mayonnaise paw prints began to appear on the microwave, and I would constantly come home to an empty fridge. She seemed like she meant well, so I politely slipped in that leaving an overturned bowl of cereal under a desk for two weeks was a health hazard. One night, she expected me to walk across campus to the library in the middle of the night because she decided to go to bed early and my "typing noises" were too loud. Thanks to the help of my very patient RA (resident advisor), I didn't pull my hair out the last weeks of the semester, and I found a new roommate for the spring. It was a huge headache to move ALL of my stuff again, but it was one of the best decisions I ever made.

— Valerie Leikina, UMass Amherst

One thing to note: if you are fortunate enough to not have to share a room with a roommate, don't think that nothing in this chapter will be helpful to you. Chances are, you'll be living in a single room within a suite or in a room off a hall where the walls are thin enough that you might as well be sharing a room with your neighbors! Cohabitation is inevitable.

> *You always hear the bad roommate stories, but this isn't one of them. My roommate and I were very close. Before school started, we e-mailed back and forth to get to know each other and became Facebook friends. At night during the school year, we would talk about being homesick, share high school stories, and argue about whose city was better. (Of course New York—my city!—won. She was from Pittsburgh.) Soon we were partying together, consulting each other for advice, and just looking out for each other! We rarely had issues, but if we needed something, we would just ask. We ended up becoming so close probably because we kept a playful atmosphere in the room and always joked around no matter what happened or what time of day or night it was.*
>
> *— Shanell Simmons, Temple University*

Keep an open mind. Don't be judgmental, and refrain from having a preconceived notion of what your roommate is going to be like. She may be completely the opposite of what you expect, or she may be just plain weird (she may act like she's from a different *planet* in your opinion), but that doesn't mean you have a right to judge her. She is a real person, just like you. In fact, she may think you are quite the odd duck yourself. Everyone has his or her idiosyncrasies; the world would be a boring place otherwise. Normality is relative—your normal may be different from hers. Appreciate who she is, as she should do for you— you never know, you might even learn a thing or two from each other.

Mid-freshman year, one of my suitemates decided to start inviting people to party in our common room—every night. The collection of half-empty bottles on our mantel ballooned, the floor developed a sticky overcoat, and a persistent damp smell permeated the room. They yelled and played loud music past 2:00 a.m. on weeknights. They copped an attitude when I appeared in pajamas from my bedroom to ask them to keep it down—then snickered after I closed the door. In retrospect, I wish I had talked to my suitemate alone, outside of the party setting. Short of that, though, it was a relief to know that my roommate shared and respected my frustration about the situation, even if the partiers mocked it. We turned our room into a safe haven and took turns policing the noise at night.

— Erica Irving, Yale University

Remember that she is just your roommate. No one ever said you had to become best friends, and in fact, it's probably better if you don't. Try to get along with her, but don't force it. If finding common ground with her turns out to be an impossible task, don't cry over it. There are SO many other things to worry about in college. Why let this one thing get to you? On the other hand, don't attach yourself to her. The two of you may decide that you are soul mates on the second day you live together, but you don't want to be glued together at the hip. The more you and your roommate depend on each other socially, the less likely you'll be motivated to go out and meet new people.

Make rules—it may seem silly, but they are necessary. Even if your roommate and you seem to be getting along swimmingly, there's no telling what button you might push later on that could really set her off. Anticipate problems, and make rules to prevent them. And if a problem arises that you didn't anticipate, make a rule to prevent it from happening again. How do you even approach a conversation about rules? Have the discussion in the midst of a mellow bonding night, perhaps when you've ordered pizza and plan on watching a movie.

Start off by telling each other about your daily habits—when you tend to go to bed and wake up, where you draw the line on sharing, how you feel about playing music, and so on. Use this conversation as a jumping-off point for creating a code of conduct and perhaps rules for anticipated conflicts. Also, agree that you will make time as needed to discuss any issues that come up—or even just to bond! Perhaps you have lunch together in the dining hall every Tuesday.

Common Roommate Conflicts

▷ **Bedtimes.** Perhaps you have an 8:00 a.m. class, and she stays up till 2:00 a.m. studying every night. If your bedtimes conflict, whoever goes to bed later should agree to keep the noise level down and the lights dim. The earlier riser should also do the same—especially turning off her alarm right away (and refraining from hitting snooze five times!) and using a hairdryer in the bathroom with the door closed. Eye masks and earplugs come in handy in these situations.

▷ **Space and sharing.** Though you are sharing a room, each of you is entitled to your own space. And it's important to note that you are in no way obligated to share your belongings with your roommate. Agree to respect each other's space and belongings, being clear about what your roommate is allowed to borrow, if anything, always asking permission first, and returning anything you borrow to its original place. If you share space or items, make sure all expenses are split evenly. If you use up your roommate's toothpaste, buy her another tube. Also, refrain from sharing items that could spread infections, like makeup, razors, and toothbrushes.

▷ **Chores and cleanliness.** Agree to clean up after yourselves, and come up with a schedule for chores. If your clothes pile up, at least make sure they stay on your side of the room, and especially be aware of odors. It's a good idea to enforce a rule that neither roommate can leave out food that can spoil—it's just bad hygiene. If you are excessively neat, be patient with a not-so-neat roommate. If you are really messy, respect your roommate's right to a clean environment.

▷ **Respecting habits, especially when it comes to noise.** Both of you may use the dorm room for different types of activities at different times. Respect each other's habits. If your roommate is studying in the room, don't bring friends over to watch TV—or at least ask if she would be bothered by the noise. If she's taking a nap, don't play loud music—use your headphones instead.

▷ **Overnight guests.** This can get pretty awkward. Decide whether overnight guests are okay with both of you, how often, and whether you need to warn the other person of an overnight visitor. Also, decide whether you want to be in the room when your roommate has an overnight guest, and vice versa. Believe it or not, if your roommate has a guest over, they might think they are being discreet while having sex (or that you are a heavy sleeper), when in reality you can hear and see everything. It can be embarrassing to talk about after it happens, so it's best to anticipate the problem and come up with an agreement. If you decide that having an overnight guest means the other roommate has to leave (called "sexiling"), come up with a set of rules.

▷ **Hosting parties.** One of you might love to host parties, while the other hates having to clean up after the guests leave or prefers a more mellow dorm environment. Come up with a compromise if this is the case—perhaps you only host parties once every couple of months or you find another locale to host them as often as you want.

━━━━━━━━━

If you have a problem with your roommate that makes it difficult for you to be comfortable in your own room, talk to her about it. After all, it is your room, too. Don't complain about her behind her back, but rather bring it up to her in a calm and reasonable manner. Be honest with her without being insulting, and be prepared to compromise or make sacrifices so both of you can be happy. Try your hardest to keep altercations and fights outside of the room—in neutral territory.

Sexiling is probably the most common roommate conflict. It has to do with shutting or kicking your roommate out of the room so you can have private time with a significant other or random hookup. First of all, discuss with your roommate whether sexiling is permissible (this is especially crucial if one of you is in a serious relationship), how often it can happen, when, and how to give each other fair warning. Come up with a system and set rules to prevent walking in on a roommate during their alone time, and also give the sexiled roommate fair enough warning so she can find another place to crash. Whether you simply agree to text each other, hang a sock on the door when you have a guest, or come up with a schedule for who gets alone time when, make sure you have a discussion about it as soon as possible—before anyone gets sexiled.

If you are having difficulty discussing conflicts with your roommate directly, involve an RA, counselor, or dean. Set up a meeting with your roommate and whoever you feel most comfortable moderating. If your roommate refuses to attend at your request, ask your counselor to intervene and maybe meet with her separately. Sometimes conflicts can get so emotional that it's better to get a third party involved to help each of you get some perspective.

Whatever you do, don't sweep things under the rug. Sometimes confronting roommate problems can seem like such a scary option, so you are tempted to just ignore the problem, keep your feelings inside, and wait till the school year ends and you can find a new roommate. While this may seem like the least confrontational option, it may cause you to build up your resentment to the extent that you hate coming home to your dorm room—the one place where you are supposed to feel safe and comfortable.

Potentially awkward or annoying roommate behaviors:

▷ Walking around naked or in a bra and panties only.

▷ Going to the bathroom with the door open or barging in without knocking.

▷ Using your roommate's stuff, borrowing her clothes, or eating her food without asking.

▷ Spending so much time in the room that your roommate doesn't get time by herself.

▷ Talking loudly on the phone all the time—especially late at night.

▷ Always coming home late really drunk and being loud.

▷ Smoking, drinking, or doing drugs in the room.

▷ Overobsessing about neatness or being a total slob.

▷ Making too much noise or turning lights on late at night or early in the morning.

▷ Having friends over when your roommate is trying to study.

▷ Napping with the lights off when your roommate needs light to study.

▷ Playing loud music or slamming doors or drawers.

▷ Allowing your friends or significant other to hang out in the room when you aren't there.

▷ Not being mindful of odors, like strong perfume or hairspray, food left out, or smelly laundry.

▷ Not turning off your alarm clock—or hitting the snooze button over and over again.

▷ Inviting guests to stay overnight without asking.

▷ Invading your roommate's privacy, like reading her e-mails on her laptop.

▷ Treating your roommate like a child—ordering her around, needing to know where she is.

▷ Allowing your roommate to pay for shared items, without contributing yourself.

I lived with five girls my sophomore year. Since we were all friends, we didn't talk about responsibilities or expectations for keeping the common space clean and comfortable for everyone. We figured that it would happen naturally, that our things would get along effortlessly, just like we did. The "live and let live" attitude worked for the first few months, but then gradually devolved into a passive-aggressive blame game when messes started piling up. The common room was only cleaned when one or two people got fed up and grumbled their way through the task. By the end of the year, one girl had become the scapegoat for this dynamic, which was really created by poor communication among all of us. Unsurprisingly, when the anger and blame spilled out, the process of choosing roommates and suitemates for the next year became way more dramatic than it needed to be.

— Erica Irving, Yale University

If things are really bad, then move out. It is a possible solution. If you complain enough (and get your parents involved), your college dean will make the arrangements for you. But use this only as a last resort. Chances are, if you communicate openly with your roommate, and involve a counselor or dean if you need to, you won't have to go to that extreme.

CHAPTER FOUR

WHY YOU ARE HERE:
THE SKINNY ON CLASSES

Choosing Classes:
Requirements versus Interests

Now that you've settled into your new home and (hopefully) started to form somewhat of a relationship with your roommate, you've got to think about classes. That *is* why you're here, remember? With everything else going on in college, somehow classes seem to get in the way. You've got new people to meet and parties to go to—who wants to waste time on *classes*? Well, the good news is, classes are going to be pretty different from the classes you took in high school. For one thing, instead of being told what subjects to take, for the most part, you'll get to take your pick. And most colleges have a pretty eclectic variety of subjects that you probably didn't even know existed. Got a fascination with underwater basket weaving? How about tree climbing? Yup, there are courses just for you!

In college you're going to spend less time staring at a talking head and putting in face time—a big plus!—but that also means you'll spend more time studying, doing problem sets, and writing papers. Less class time translates to more independent work, which equals a whole lot of self-discipline. It may take a while to get used to the demands of college life on top of your academics, but believe me, it is possible. Once you've got the juggling act down—as you bounce around from party to study group to club meeting to class—you'll embrace the constant stimulation. After all, it could only mean you're making the absolute most of your college experience.

"You mean I get to decide what classes to take?" Hard to believe, I know. For the most part, you do, as long as you: 1) fulfill your school's course requirements, 2) meet the requirements for your intended major, and 3) take enough classes to qualify you to earn your degree. These criteria are usually not hard to comply with, and they are great guidelines for ensuring that once you graduate you are not only well rounded with a solid general education, but also thoroughly knowledgeable in one particular subject area—both very important qualities when you enter the job market.

At some colleges, during your first year, your advisor creates your schedule for you. If this is the case, your school probably has a ton of core or distribution requirements that you need to fulfill right away. Don't fret—once you take those required classes, you can take your pick later on. One thing's for sure, at some point you'll get to choose your classes, and it can be a pretty exciting—and overwhelming—endeavor. There are so many options! How do you even begin?

Unusual (and Actual!) College Courses

Who wants to learn about British poetry when you can take a class on everything you need to know about trash? Believe it or not, the following courses actually exist—maybe even at a college near you:

1. *The Art of Walking* (Centre College). Not a how-to, but rather a why-not, this course is for "people who can walk, but don't," using the philosophy of Kant to encourage students to explore nature through this lost art.
2. *Sex, Rugs, Salt, and Coal* (Cornell University). Examining the changing environmental and cultural impacts of market forces, this class answers questions like, "How was the taste of sugar linked to the slave trade?" and "Is prostitution really the oldest profession?"
3. *The Joy of Garbage* (Santa Clara University). Students explore the processes of decomposition and waste, as well as social justice issues, such as why landfills are frequently located in poorer neighborhoods. Who knew trash could be so fascinating?
4. *The Phallus* (Occidental College). This critical theory and social justice class discusses topics such as the relationship between the

phallus and the penis, the lesbian phallus, and phallogocentrism.

5. *Maple Syrup: The Real Thing* (Alfred University). In this class not only do students learn about the profession and process of making this delicious topping, but also recipes that use it—yum. The class also includes a field trip! Could it get any better than that?

6. *Learning from YouTube* (Pitzer College). Watch YouTube videos, discuss said videos, comment on said videos—that's pretty much the gist of it. And all class materials, including the syllabus, are on YouTube (www.youtube.com/group/learningfromyoutube).

7. *Examining Urban Crime, Policing, Politics, and Delinquency in* The Wire (Loyola University). Who wouldn't love a class in which all five seasons of what has been referred to by many as "the best show on television" are actually considered *required "reading"*?

8. *Underwater Basket Weaving* (Reed College). The title pretty much says it all. And Reed's not the only one: University of Arizona offers the similar, but much more specific *Submerged Snorkeling Basket Weaving.*

9. *Finding Dates Worth Keeping* (University of Sioux Falls). You can't go wrong with a class whose content you can apply to everyday life! Among other things, you'll learn how to date and when to break up—the essentials!

10. *Tree Climbing* (Cornell University). This course allows students to fulfill the school's physical education requirement simply by learning how to climb trees, as well as how to move around in them and climb from one to the other.

Get those distribution requirements out of the way. Most colleges have distribution, or core, requirements, which means you are expected to take either specific classes or a few classes distributed among designated subject areas. Core requirements encourage you to take courses in a wide variety of disciplines, while still giving you the freedom to choose (however creatively!) within those areas. For example, you could fulfill a physical education requirement by taking anything from

Bowling to Tree Climbing. Or maybe one of your four required math or hard science classes could be Amusement Park Physics. If your school has core requirements, consider getting them out of the way as soon as possible. Doing so forces you to investigate subjects you may not have considered otherwise, ensuring you are well informed come the end of sophomore year when you have to declare your major (and minor, if you so choose). Then you can spend the last two years focusing on your true interests and taking some fun electives on the side.

Consider a few major requirements. Don't worry if you have no idea what you want to major in yet. Most incoming students haven't got a clue! At most colleges you aren't required to declare a major until the end of your sophomore year, so you'll have a couple of years to decide. Take full advantage of all that time, always keeping an open mind and embracing the opportunity to dabble. However, if you have even the tiniest inkling of what you might be passionate about, consider taking a required class or two in that major, especially if there are prerequisites. (A *prerequisite* is an introductory or survey course that you must take before enrolling in a higher-level course.) For example, if you're considering majoring in English, and you know the Major English Poets seminar is a prerequisite, take it as soon as your schedule allows. That way, if you declare yourself an English major sophomore year, you'll be free to take whatever English courses you want, having gotten the prerequisite out of the way. Some math- or science-heavy majors, such as premed, engineering, or business, are prereq-intensive. So in the event that you are interested in any of these or similar majors, it's a good idea to start taking a few of those prerequisites early on. Otherwise, during your freshman year, just take a combination of classes that both interest and challenge you. Keep an eye out for a possible subject to focus on, but don't make any solid decisions yet—enjoy this opportunity to be free of obligation!

Take those course descriptions with a grain of salt. Those one-paragraph overviews don't mean much, as every professor could teach the same course differently. You'll get a better sense of the course by seeking out the inside scoop. Talk to upperclassmen who have already taken it; they'll give you the uncensored story on what the class is really like. If you have no idea what to take at all, ask upperclassmen for some recommendations based on your interests (however vague they might be) or lifestyle (e.g., afternoon lecture classes as opposed to morning seminars). Also, many schools provide online course reviews written by students. Find out if your school has them, and use them as a guide while choosing classes.

My first semester of college I was a pre-nursing major, but I didn't take the time to think about whether I really enjoyed nursing. I only took into consideration that it was a financially stable career with good benefits. This was a big mistake; I didn't enjoy any of the classes I was taking. Thankfully, there was one required class, Intro to Psychology, which I completely fell in love with. I quickly switched my major to psychology and have been in love with the field ever since. If you are not completely sure about what you want to major in, take a variety of classes your first semester in order to broaden your horizons and see what else is out there. College is about finding out who you are as a person and what your interests are.

— Jennifer Conde, University of South Florida

The professor makes the course. Ask around about good professors. If you're like me, the course content doesn't matter as much as how engaging the professor is. A class called The Psychology of Human Intimacy sounds fascinating, but not if the professor drones on and on until the entire lecture hall has been lulled to sleep. Many college students find websites like RateMyProfessors.com and ProfessorPerformance.com helpful in getting student opinions on specific professors. View these sites with caution, however, as often the reviews emphasize whether a professor is an easy grader, rather than quality of instruction—and hopefully the latter is more important to you than the former! Also, there's no way of knowing if these anonymous evaluations are legitimate; they are sometimes used by students to get revenge after receiving a poor grade. Refrain from letting a review on one of these websites make or break your decision—let it be one of many factors in choosing your classes.

The debate on "gut" courses. To take them or not to take them? "Gut" or "bird" courses are referred to as such because they're easy and you can just fly right through them. On the one hand, taking such pushover courses allows you to concentrate on the more important ones in your schedule and eke out a little more of a social life. On the other hand, you are paying a lot of money for an education, so why waste time on pointless classes? The verdict: taking an easy class once in a while can't hurt, as long as you are at least moderately interested in the material. Don't take a class in a subject you despise just because it's famed to be an easy course. In fact, it may not be so easy for you because of your lack of interest in the subject matter. And sometimes professors find out about the fame of their gut courses and suddenly decide to make the classes much more difficult.

The best way to get to know a professor's teaching style is to talk to the professor yourself. The best ones would be happy to converse with anyone who's interested in their area of expertise—in fact, many professors love to listen to themselves talk! Pay a visit during office hours (times designated for student walk-ins), and ask about the class. After a fifteen-minute conversation—during which you are appropriately engaged and curious—you'll have a pretty good sense of what the professor is like in the classroom.

Form an opinion on format. Most schools have three different class formats: lecture, seminar, and online. Each format caters to a different type of learning style, so if you're not quite sure how you'll learn best, try taking a class or two in each format. To get a good sense of how they differ, check out the following chart.

Class Type	Lecture
Size	25–200 or more
Discussion	Lecture is often supplemented by a small discussion section that meets for an extra hour per week and is led by a teaching assistant.
Level and Depth	Usually survey or introductory course covering a wide range of material without going into too much depth.
Reading	Requires self-discipline to complete it, as you usually aren't tested on the material until the final exam (don't cram!).
Professor Interaction	Less interaction with the professor and more interaction with the teaching assistant.
Attendance	Less important, unless the professor keeps track. If you miss a class, you can usually get the notes from someone else or learn from the reading, or the professor may post lecture notes online.
Mode of Learning	You take notes in class and then pick and choose what to read from the assigned reading depending on what the professor stresses.
Basis for Grading	You will most likely have a final exam covering the most pertinent information.
Best Suited for Those Who:	• Prefer to learn a little about a lot. • Learn best through a combination of reading and listening. • Would rather listen than talk or write. • Have moderate self-discipline.

Seminar	Online
6–25	Varies
The class itself is in discussion format, in which the students talk about the material with the professor or a teaching assistant as mediator.	Discussion of the material takes place online, usually in discussion boards located on the class's website.
Usually higher-level course covering less material in greater depth.	Varies, though usually higher-level course covering less material in greater depth.
You have no choice but to keep up with most of the reading if you want to appear knowledgeable in class discussion.	Since all discussions occur online, you might be able to get away with minimal reading, as long as you read enough to complete assignments.
More interaction with the professor since the class is so much smaller.	All interaction with the professor is virtual.
Extremely important, as your participation is important to your grade. If you're not there, you can't discuss the material, which is how you are evaluated in class.	Though there is no physical class to attend, you may be required to be online at certain times for discussion or to turn in weekly assignments as a way of showing consistent involvement.
You learn the material by discussing whatever you and your classmates are interested in examining further.	You learn the material through online discussions with your classmates, as well as through frequent, shorter writing assignments.
You will most likely have to write a final paper in which you develop your own argument based on the material that interests you.	Varies—you could have weekly written assignments and then a final paper, or you may take a final exam online (usually open book, with a time limit).
• Prefer to learn a lot about a little. • Learn best through a combination of reading and discussion. • Would rather talk than listen or write. • Have a great deal of self-discipline.	• Prefer to learn a lot about a little. • Learn best through a combination of reading and writing. • Would rather write than listen or talk. • Have a TON of self-discipline.

Pay attention to the fine print. Class dates and times, exam dates, assignment due dates, and any final exams or papers that may be required—keep all these factors in mind when deciding on your class schedule. If you fare better on papers than you do on exams, take classes that require only papers. If you're not so much a morning person, only take classes in the afternoon. If you need more than just one day to study for a final exam, schedule your classes so that your final exams are spread out through exam week. One of the best things about college is that you actually have these kinds of options.

Attend the class first before you decide, if possible. Some colleges have a "shopping period," lasting a week or two, during which you can shop different classes first before you figure out your final schedule. If your school allows for this, take advantage of it. Shop as many classes as you can in order to get a feel for the professor, the workload, and whether you are even interested in the topic. If you don't have this freedom, register for one or two more classes than necessary and drop the ones you ultimately lose interest in. (Make sure you drop them before your school's drop deadline, so you don't end up with a big "Incomplete" on your transcript.) Alternatively, if you're unsure about a particular class, take it "for credit" (pass/fail) instead of for a grade, if your school offers this option. In the event that you love the course and thus are doing well, you can change it to a grade mid-semester.

Ask and you will receive! As a freshman, I didn't make it through the lottery for a very popular English class, and only one spot was left untaken. The next day at least twenty of us showed up for this one coveted spot. Rather than waiting for things to sort themselves out, I took the suggestion of an upperclassman and went to the English Department to request to be the person to take this one spot. The man at the desk looked at me, thought a moment and replied, "You're nice enough. Sure! The spot is yours."

— Courtney Grafton, Yale University

If you really want to get into a popular class that has limited enrollment, talk your way into it. Believe it or not, it works about 75 percent of the time. Talk to the professor or send an e-mail showing your enthusiasm for the course. Say that you've read the professor's work and are planning on writing your senior thesis on a related topic. Assert that you are considering majoring in the department and you believe this class will help you decide. If you're persistent enough, you'll get what you want. Smile a lot, too. It can only help your chances.

> Try the "sit-in" technique. Sophomore year, I went into spring semester registered for only one class. I had a hold on my account, and by the time I got it straightened out, all the classes I needed were filled. So... I just attended them anyway. At the end of each class, I explained the situation to the professor and asked to be overridden into the class. Fortunately, at my school the maximum enrollment quantity is set significantly lower than the room can actually hold. Even at maximum "capacity," they can make room for an extra student or two because, chances are, the only time everyone enrolled comes to class is during an exam.
>
> — Valerie Leikina, UMass Amherst

Start off with a light course load. You've got so many adjustments to make your first semester; the least you can do for yourself is keep classes down to a minimal stress level. And remember, you're supposed to be making friends at this point, so it's best not to lock yourself in the library all day to study for six or seven classes. Consider starting easy—or at least balance out some difficult classes with some light ones. Once you get used to college academics, you can slowly challenge yourself more and more. Sophomore and junior year, you can pile on the harder classes. By then you'll have a solid circle of friends who won't turn their backs when you need to hit the books.

On the other hand, if academics are your absolute priority, you are confident you can handle seven classes, and you could care less about a social life, by all means, take seven classes! Just know how much you can handle without spreading yourself too thin, and remember that you also need time to eat and sleep. Be prepared to face skepticism from advisors who will discourage you from taking more than five classes a semester.

Surviving Classes: Studying and Time Management

Once you've chosen your classes, the next thing to do is figure out how to survive them. This involves managing your time, adopting good study habits, and learning how to write papers effectively. And if you can't do any of these things very well (which may be the case your first semester), earning decent grades may involve cramming and pulling all-nighters. But let's hope you don't reach that point—those kinds of poor study habits won't benefit you in the long run. And by the time you finish this chapter, you should be well equipped to manage your time well, hopefully ensuring that you will never have to pull an all-nighter during your four years at college.

Become well acquainted with each class's virtual learning environment (VLE). Almost all colleges and universities nowadays are using VLEs or online course management systems (CMS) to facilitate professor-student communication and exchange of materials, as well as to supplement (or replace) classroom learning. VLEs allow professors to post all class materials for students to access, including syllabi, presentation slides, lecture notes, readings, assignments, exams, and even grades. In turn, students are expected to submit their assignments and also engage in online class discussions via this course management system. So if your school uses such a platform—it probably has a clever moniker like "ClassWeb" or "Classes*v2"—make sure you know how to use it! These VLEs are usually pretty user-friendly, but if you need some help learning how to navigate yours, don't be afraid to ask a fellow student or IT (information technology) specialist to guide you through it. Once you master the VLE, you'll see how it can make your academic life much easier, as it includes other special features like calendars and reminders. Take advantage of it!

If your school doesn't use a VLE, chances are your professors will rely heavily on e-mail to communicate with their students, so be sure to check your e-mail often.

Textbooks. You'll soon discover that textbooks could easily cost hundreds of dollars a semester, especially if you buy them new and from the school's bookstore. Don't buy new textbooks. Buy them used or from websites like Half.com or Amazon.com. Better yet, rent them from your school's bookstore if they have such a program, or rent from sites like CampusBookRentals.com or Chegg.com. If you are ordering online, make sure to order early enough so the book is shipped to you before you have to complete the first assigned reading. Another option is purchasing the e-book version of your textbook if it comes in this format and if you have an e-reader. The e-book formats tend to be significantly cheaper than hard-copy books since they are electronic files. (For more about saving on textbooks, see Chapter 8.)

When you're buying used, make sure you are purchasing the correct edition of the book. Some textbooks change dramatically between editions, so make sure you are getting the right one!

Go to class—and participate! It may seem silly to remind you to actually attend your classes (especially if you were a really good student in high school), but you'll see: once you get there and find yourself swept up in college craziness, the idea of skipping class will become more and more conceivable to you. Plus, technology and the Internet have made it possible to cut class and retrieve all the information you missed later. Many professors post their lecture slides and notes online, or they may even use tablet PCs to write electronic notes on their slides and record their lectures for students to watch online later. In fact, many colleges create electronic recordings of all class lectures that are available immediately for student access. And if these options aren't available, you can always borrow notes from one of your classmates. So, you ask, why attend class at all? First of all, for most courses, class attendance and participation make up a certain percentage of your grade. Many professors or their teaching assistants (TAs) not only take attendance, but also keep track of the number of times you speak in class. At some colleges, profs use an electronic response unit, like EduClick, in their lecture classes. In this system, students use an electronic answer remote to register their attendance, reply to professors' questions anonymously and instantaneously, or give answers to tests.

If the thought of speaking in class causes you to break out in hives, you're not alone! Fortunately, class participation usually only accounts for a portion of your total grade, so you can make up for it by writing phenomenal papers and killing your exams. In case you still need that extra 10 percent participation grade to bump up your B+ to an A, try the following tactics:

1. To avoid the pressure of speaking off-the-cuff, come to each seminar ready with a comment on the readings to start off the discussion. Your prof will be impressed with your initiative, and you won't have to speak again for the rest of the class period.

2. Whenever anyone else is speaking, nod enthusiastically and sprinkle in a few *uh-huh*s and *good point!*s and *I never considered that!*s every so often.

3. When you can't think of anything original to say, simply repeat or confirm what was just said, using different words. (For example, PROF: So, to sum up, the Earth is round. STUDENT: In other words, it isn't flat?)

For the sake of your academic and career success, it's also a good idea to put in a lot of face time with your professors. Participating in class will not only help your grade, but also get you noticed. And it's extremely important that you start to develop relationships with them as soon as you can, as from these relationships can come mentorships and letters of recommendation for future internships and jobs, as well as advice and support through college, your career, and your life. As I've said, in college you learn the most outside the classroom, and that includes those connections and interactions that you foster with faculty members.

Master the art of in-class note taking. Whether you're better with handwritten or typed notes, get to know what works for you. Hand writing your notes is probably easier in a class like economics or physics where you have to write down a ton of diagrams and figures. Otherwise, most students prefer bringing a laptop to class and typing their notes, as they are then able to store and share them easily. If you do bring your laptop, keep your browser and all other applications closed so you're not tempted to peruse Facebook or surf the web during the lecture. (Actually, many profs don't allow students to use their laptops because of such Internet distractions.) If the professor posts lecture slides online before class, don't forget to download them to your laptop or print them out beforehand, so you can type or write your notes directly on them. When taking notes, concentrate on recording the professor's explanations rather than on copying down the slides (if you don't have them in class, you can probably get them later). And try to develop your own shorthand— use letters, symbols, colors, whatever works—early on to make note taking more efficient.

Know all your due dates, deadlines, and exam dates. On the first day of class, your professors will each provide you with a syllabus that includes the class schedule, requirements, and assigned readings. Keep track on your calendar when every paper is due and every test is scheduled. Label every oral presentation and every problem set due date. If you use the calendar app on your laptop or mobile device, make sure to also program it to notify you when a deadline or exam is approaching. In fact, have it remind you repeatedly at various points if you think you'll need to be nagged to stay on track. Or go old school and write the due dates on a wall calendar and then hang it up right above your desk or anywhere you won't be able to avoid looking at it. Hopefully the sight of the huge red marks on days fast approaching will scare you into getting your act together for the next assignment or exam.

Keep up with all those online assignments. Even if you're not taking an online course, many of your classes will require you to complete assignments online. Some profs regularly post discussion topics on the discussion boards within their VLEs and require each student to comment on these topics. Or you may be required to post weekly responses to class readings before coming to class. Alternatively, many profs require students to write a weekly blog on the class material. Whatever the case, stay on top of these online assignments, as they often make up the class participation grade.

The Top 5 Ways "A" Students End Up with a C+

1. *Missing too many classes*—whether it's because of extracurriculars or hangovers.
2. *Not talking enough in class.* Even if you're shy, just say *something* or at least nod as though you're interested.
3. *Getting on the prof's bad side*, like writing a paper that blatantly disagrees with his or her ideas.
4. *Asking for too many due-date extensions.* If you make a habit of it, your prof will think you don't care.
5. *Waiting till the last minute to start your research paper and finding all the books you need are gone.* Even if you aren't planning on writing your paper until the night before, at *least* get the books in advance!

Set your own mini-deadlines each week, and give yourself more time than you think you need. The more time you spend in school and managing classes, you'll start to get to know yourself and how much time you need for writing papers, doing problem sets, and studying for exams—if you don't have a good sense of that already. If you know that you'll need a good eight days to write a decent eight-page literary analysis on Shakespeare's *The Tempest*, then get to work on it eight days before it's due, perhaps with the goal of writing one page a day. If you've got an entire semester to write a twenty-page research paper on the Cold War, allot a certain number of weeks for research, a certain number for drafting, and the last week for editing and revision. Always give yourself more time than you think you need. You never know what might come up, so it's better to get a head start. You may be halfway done with a paper and suddenly want to change your topic. You may want to meet with your professor to get some feedback on where you're headed with your research. Heck, on the day before your paper is due, your roommate might have a crisis and need you to come to the rescue. You never know!

Stay on top of required readings! Every professor always assigns about three times as much reading as a normal human being is actually capable of doing. Chances are, you don't actually have to read everything. Your professor will likely tell you which readings are essential and which are just optional or supplemental. If they don't, ask! You're probably not the only student who wants to know. Regardless of whether all the readings are actually required, always read as much as you can. You'll have the most fulfilling learning experience, and you will be better informed during class discussions, when writing papers, and when taking exams.

If you're having trouble keeping up, try these strategies:

▷ **Skim.** Read the introduction, the first and last sentences of every paragraph, and the conclusion. This gives you a general idea of the material and is most effective in classes that evaluate you with exams rather than papers. Use caution with this tactic if your professor gives very detailed tests. Find out which readings you will be tested on, and read those thoroughly.

▷ **Read selectively.** Read a few well-chosen texts in depth. This way, you don't know all the material, but rather a few important things in very good detail. Ask the prof, TA, or previous students which texts are essential, hone in on the ones the prof emphasizes in the lecture or seminar, or choose the texts that are most relevant to the written assignments. This approach works best for classes that evaluate based on class participation or analytical papers. If you are able to discuss a few key points in class, the professor will assume that you have done all the necessary reading.

▷ **Take notes on the readings.** Even if you can't read everything, make sure you are actually absorbing what you are able to read. Many students find that taking notes on the readings is helpful, as that added act of rewriting the information after reading it aids in recall. If this seems too time consuming, at least highlight or underline the key points or write brief notes in the margins.

Study in different places. At a café. In the bookstore. In a coffee shop. On a bench outside. In the student lounge. On the grass. At the local diner. In the dining hall. In an empty classroom. On the bleachers. In a courtyard. On a hammock. In a library study room. On a swing. On a rooftop.

Study in an environment that's comfortable, but not too comfortable. During your first semester at college, try studying in different environments to figure out which one allows you to get work done more effectively. Know yourself and how much or how little noise you prefer in your work environment. And, if at all possible, avoid studying in your room. Your room is where you sleep, where you hang out, and where there are lots of distractions.

> *I move my study location almost every time I do work. It depends on my mood. If I'm feeling social I'll go to the library, or if I don't want to run into anyone who will distract me, I'll find an empty classroom in an academic building and work there. But no matter where I'm studying, I always make sure I have a bottle of water, my iPod, sticky notes, highlighters, and a snack. That way I can focus without wishing I had brought something else with me.*
>
> *— Carolyn Spalding, Lafayette College*

Pace yourself so you don't have to cram or pull an all-nighter later. Every one of your classes will load you with an enormous amount of reading, and it will be impossible to do all of it the night before the exam. Cramming is never fun, and it's easy to avoid if you do the reading you're supposed to do for each week. Honestly, if you start at the beginning of the semester, spending just two hours in the library studying every day, you will have less cramming to do come final exam time.

The best scenario is to not let all-nighters happen. You shouldn't have to, especially if you manage your time wisely. Staying up all night to write a paper or study for an exam is not good for your health, and it will probably result in a mediocre paper or exam grade. That said, I know that at first it's really hard to learn how to manage your time. So it's possible that you will have no choice but to pull an all-nighter at least once. If this is the case for you, let that one time be the only time; think of it as your one get-out-of-jail-free card. It's no fun, so then shape up and get your act together from that point on.

Stay away from study drugs. On college campuses, many students are frequently using what are often called "study drugs," prescription stimulant medications like Adderall and Ritalin, to help them stay awake to study. The abuse of these drugs has become prevalent because they are not only easy to obtain through prescription but also through illegal distribution. These drugs make pulling an all-nighter seem like an easy task. Because they can be legally prescribed, students convince themselves that using these drugs is safe and acceptable—especially since they are being used for staying up to study, rather than recreationally. *Don't, under any circumstances, use these or any other prescription drugs unless they were prescribed to you, and if they were, only use them according to the doses dictated by your doctor. If you have been prescribed any drugs, do not share them with other people.*

If you do have to pull an all-nighter, keep these tips in mind:

▷ **Get into the right mindset.** You've reached this point, and now you have no choice but to follow through. So commit to staying up all night, and plan on sticking to it.

▷ **Position yourself.** Choose a well-lit, comfortable (but not too comfortable) area with minimal distraction and by an open window—not your bed (where you'll be tempted to nap) and not the student lounge (where you'll be tempted to socialize). The window's fresh air should keep you alert. Stay off the Internet—or if you need it to study, DON'T go on Facebook.

▷ **Arm yourself with snacks, cold water, and caffeine (as a last resort).** Trail mix, peanut M&Ms, or anything crunchy. Cold water to drink (and splash on your face) works better than caffeine (without the crash!)—and getting up to go to the bathroom often ensures you won't fall asleep.

▷ **Study with a buddy or while listening to soft music if neither will distract you.** To prevent you from konking out, enlist a study buddy who will stay on task and keep you awake.

▷ **Take short but frequent study breaks.** Consider these breaks your small rewards. Try ten minutes every hour, or twenty minutes every two hours. Do something active, like walking around or jumping jacks. Use a few of those breaks to switch locations, too, to keep you from getting too comfortable. Set an alarm on your cell phone so your study breaks don't last longer than the time allotted.

▷ **Envision your ultimate, final reward.** To get you through the night, plan on rewarding yourself with something other than the completed paper and a long nap. Let it be something really mouthwatering—like a really big and delicious breakfast at the local diner.

A quick study break can do wonders for your progress. Make yourself a snack. Lift weights. Play solitaire. Pluck your eyebrows. Get a slice of pizza. Chat online (but not for too long—don't get hooked!). Download some music. Bake brownies. Take a shower. Write a letter. Have a five-minute dance party. Get some ice cream. Play a video game. Think of things to invent so you can be rich. Google your name. Daydream. Do some yoga. Watch one episode of your favorite TV show online. Take a walk. Visit friends. Make a to-do list. Sing loudly. Stretch. Visit your favorite blog.

> *The thing I found hardest to avoid when staying up all night was that little voice that chimes in saying, "Maybe I'll just nap for a couple hours. I'm not doing myself any good studying half asleep anyway." It was never a nap, and I never actually woke up and resumed studying. I went to those tests unprepared and came home with a less-than-satisfactory grade. I learned that procrastination has its price. If I put myself in that situation, I better tough it out and go all the way.*
>
> *— Valerie Leikina, UMass Amherst*

Know when a study group is helpful—and when it's harmful. Study groups can make studying much more fun and less stressful, but they can also be a waste of time—it depends on your personality and the subject matter. Study groups can be extremely helpful in subjects like physics, engineering, and organic chemistry, because the group can work together to figure out difficult concepts and formulas more quickly. Just make sure you do a ton of studying on your own first before participating in a study group. If you think of the study group as your only source of preparation for an exam, you may be expecting too much.

Use your first paper assignment as a gauge. Every professor grades differently and every professor stresses a different aspect of the analytical essay, whether it is the strength of the argument, the clarity of writing, the writing style, or the strength of the evidence. Once you've been graded on your first paper, you'll get a sense of what the professor is looking for. If you are disappointed with your grade—or any other grade for that matter—don't whine about it and don't be afraid to ask your professor why you received it. Also, ask if you can revise the paper for a better grade—many profs will give you a second chance. (See page 23 for a list of useful style and grammar guides.)

It's all in the title. The title of an essay can make or break your grade. Well, not really, but almost all your professors will want you to have a title, and it's important that the title is indicative of the quality of your paper. Thankfully, there's actually a formula for this, and you can even come up with a title long before you've written the paper itself! To create a paper title, use the [X]: [Y] in [Z] model. In this model:

X is a quote or phrase from the work or from some other literary resource, at least slightly relevant to your topic.

Y is the subject matter you're writing about.

Z is the name of the author or text you're writing about.

Example: "Your Scent Is like a Drug to Me": Manipulation and Addiction in Meyer's *Twilight*.

Don't be afraid to ask for help. Your professors and TAs are there for a reason. Don't be scared by your professors, as intimidating as they might be. They were once freshmen, too. And you can also ask your classmates, campus tutors, or even the cute boy who sits in front of you for some assistance. Hmm, maybe the two of you can work together on the next problem set.

Make sure you back up all your papers and written assignments on a hard drive, a thumb drive, or better yet, a server. Store them in multiple locations so you will never lose them.

CHAPTER FIVE

HEALTH AND WELLNESS: TAKING CARE OF YOURSELF

Picture this: You have just rolled out of bed for your 8:30 a.m. class. Your hair is in a knotted ponytail, there are dark circles under your glassy eyes, and you're fumbling across campus in jeans that used to fit but now feel a little tight thanks to the extra two inches around your waist that also seem to be slowing your pace to class. You could care less. Whatever. Lately you've been doing great in school thanks to your routine of back-to-back all-nighters, and they give you free soda at the local pizza place since you go there so often for your late-night study breaks. Life is *good*, you think to yourself. You're surprised you somehow managed to mentally string these three words together in your near-comatose state, as you jam your favorite powdered doughnut down your throat and wash it down with some black coffee.

It's not a pretty sight, but it's a sight that's not so rare for the typical college student. You get so wrapped up in the juggling act that you forget to show love to the person who needs it the most: the juggler—you. Without her, everything falls to the floor. Remember: with all the changes that will take place in your life over the next four years, the one thing that will always remain constant is you. So take care of yourself—physically, mentally, and emotionally. College life is hard enough already. Don't make it harder by depriving yourself of sleep, exercise, and a healthy diet. Maintaining your health—both physical and mental—is essential to being in top form for maximizing your college experience.

First things first: let's talk about the "freshman fifteen." According to this widely held belief, every freshman in college gains fifteen pounds by the time the year comes to a close. But this is a myth. The truth is that college is a time of fluctuation in weight and overall health for many people, but the freshman fifteen is not universal.

In your first year of college, you will be going through many changes, including changes in the way you eat, how much you exercise, and how you take care of your body. With the new responsibilities of independence and the anxiety that may accompany such a huge life transition, both you and your body could respond in a variety of ways. Focus on exercising, eating healthily, and taking care of your body so you can love the person you are no matter how much you weigh.

> I refused to believe I could possibly gain fifteen pounds in one school year. I was wrong—I gained fifteen pounds in a semester! The cookies, buffet dinners, and fast-food restaurants—available at my convenience—all ensured I wasn't going to burn enough calories around the track to maintain my body weight. Slowly the slim figure I had started to thicken. My favorite jeans didn't fit anymore. I wasn't fond of the way I looked. I knew I had to change—but I knew change wouldn't come overnight. So I started to get comfortable in my skin as I attempted to eat less—and healthier!—and exercise more. By the end of the summer I was back to my original weight. More importantly, I learned to love my body enough to take good care of it, regardless of the number on the scale. AND I came into sophomore year with a new hairstyle and a new attitude!
>
> — Nicole White, Purdue University

And one more thing, before we move on: make friends with your school's student health center. College student health centers get a bad rap. As the story goes, whatever your reason for paying a visit, even if it's just for a head cold, you will be told that either you have mono or you could be pregnant. Who knows how they got that reputation, but it's somehow spread to student health centers at colleges all across the country. Don't believe this nonsense. Truth be told, your student health center will be a great resource for all things health related, so it's a good idea to get to know your primary care doctor, and even make friends with a few of the nurses. You'll be dealing with a lot in college, and chances are you'll have trouble staying healthy on top of everything else. Your student health center will probably be a frequent stop on your college journey—whether you've gotten the flu from your roommate, you need a new contact lens prescription, you're looking for a counselor to talk to, or you want to learn about your birth control options (see Chapter 7). Get to know the practitioners there so you know who to turn to no matter what you need help with.

Get Some Sleep!

Make sleep a priority. College students never seem to get enough sleep. There's so much to do in college, and now that you don't have Mom and Dad enforcing curfews, you've got eight or so more hours to schedule as you see fit. But this doesn't mean that using those hours for some quality sleep isn't the most effective use of time. You need to get enough sleep to think straight and survive your classes. You need to get enough sleep to function—period.

At first, you'll be so busy trying to fit everyone and everything into your schedule that sleep will be the last thing on your priority list. Then you will start to *crave* it. You'll fall asleep in class and use every free minute you have during the day for a nap. Replacing a full night's sleep with intermittent daytime naps will just turn you into a zombie. Ultimately, getting all the sleep you need at one time, at the right time (nighttime), will ensure you get the most out of it. If you must take a nap, make it short—twenty to thirty minutes—and set an alarm so you don't miss class, rehearsal, or a meeting.

Plan ahead so you can get things done while still getting the sleep you need. Like I've said many times throughout this book already, it all boils down to time management (see Chapters 4 and 8). As you begin to take control of your time and schedule all your classes, activities, and other important engagements, make sleep a part of that schedule. In fact, if it will help, put it in your calendar as a repeating event, so that your mobile device notifies you at, say, 11:00 p.m. every night when you should be getting ready for bed (especially if you have a

9:00 a.m. class). Aim to get eight hours of sleep every night—unfortunately, many college students only get between three and five hours.

━━━━━━━━━

Can't sleep? Let's face it, even if you dutifully crawl into bed at 11:30 p.m. with every intention of falling right to sleep and getting those eight glorious and well-deserved hours of slumber—there's always a chance that you'll be faced with one of many obstacles that are just part and parcel of college life. Here are a few examples of such sleep enemies and some ideas for defeating them:

▷ **Nocturnal roommate.** It's tough to get to bed when your roommate's typing away on her laptop and listening to her pumped-for-an-all-nighter playlist. Try proposing the following compromise: a few nights a week she studies in the student lounge so you can get your beauty sleep; the other few nights you wear earplugs and an eye mask—and she uses her headphones. (For more on resolving roommate conflicts, see Chapter 3.)

▷ **Overcaffeinated.** Love your coffee? Most college students do, especially those who are sleep deprived and need a constant pick-me-up. If you're having trouble falling asleep, though, the culprit might be that cup of coffee you had after dinner or even the chocolate you inhaled during your last study break. To ensure a good night's sleep, refrain from any caffeinated food or drink at least three hours before bedtime.

▷ **Stressed out!** The life of a college girl is rarely stress free. There's just so much going on—class, rehearsal, love life, roommate drama! So perhaps you find yourself tossing and turning at night with your mind racing. Before you hit the sack, write down everything you are worried about—better yet, make a to-do list for the following day. Emptying your head of stressful thoughts before bedtime can help calm your mind and welcome sleep.

▷ **A few nightcaps too many.** Although alcohol is supposed to be a relaxant, having a few drinks at night can often have the opposite effect of keeping you up—especially if you are already kind of stressed out. If you think this might be the case for you, don't drink any alcohol at least a couple of hours before it's time for bed.

▷ **Party going on next door.** Leave it to your neighbors to find a reason to party on a Monday night. If those earplugs don't do the trick, feel free to knock on their door and ask them to keep it down. If the volume level goes back up again after ten minutes, complain to your RA. Lucky for you, your right to a good night's sleep supersedes their right to party.

Exercise!

So we've now ensured that you are well rested and thus have sufficient energy reserves for the daily pressures of college life. The next step is to build up your strength and endurance not only to get you in shape, but also to keep you sharp and focused. If you played sports or had physical education classes in high school, exercise was probably a part of your daily routine, so you didn't have to do much else besides follow orders from your coach or PE teacher to stay in moderate shape. Well, in college, physical fitness won't be as automated: you'll be in complete control of how, when, and where you exercise, and you'll have to be your own coach when it comes to staying motivated.

Make exercise a part of your daily routine. Discipline yourself to work out every day. It may be difficult at first, so try taking baby steps: start with once or twice a week; then after a month, increase to three or four times, and so on. Once you've worked out every day for a month or so, it will become a habit. In fact, you'll feel how your body changes whenever you miss a workout. Make exercise a necessity—a fixed part of your schedule just as important as going to class. If you like consistency, work out at the same time every day. If you tend to get bored easily, vary your workout times to keep things interesting. If you tend to make excuses for skipping a workout, exercise early in the day so you get it over with. Actually, a morning workout is more effective and better for you than a caffeine jolt. Exercise gives you energy, which will fuel your body for the rest of the day. On the other hand, many find that working out in the evening is a great stress release after a long day. Find out what works for you.

Workouts don't always have to be planned. Exercise if you need a study break or if you are feeling stressed out. Head to the gym or go for a run if you've got an hour to kill between classes or if other plans got cancelled.

All you need is thirty minutes a day. A lot of people are hesitant to work out because they think they have to sacrifice a huge chunk of time from their day to do it. Start out at just thirty minutes every day, and aim to slowly increase your workout time—say by five minutes each week—to an hour. To keep things interesting, alternate between cardiovascular workouts and weight lifting.

Get a workout buddy. If you have trouble motivating yourself to work out, exercise with a friend. This way you can keep each other in check. You'll also be less likely to skip a workout if you've got someone else to answer to.

Vary your workouts so you don't get bored. Perhaps on Monday evening you run on the treadmill, Tuesday morning you use the weight machines, Wednesday afternoon you throw around a Frisbee on the quad, Thursday morning you go for a bike ride around campus, Friday evening you take a kickboxing class, Saturday morning you practice yoga, and Sunday evening you play in an intramural soccer game. Working out sounds kind of fun when it's something different every day, doesn't it? Changing it up gives you something new to look forward to and also allows you to exercise different parts of your body. Get creative and have fun!

Don't be afraid to go to the gym. As a student at your college, you're already paying to have access to the gym, so you might as well take advantage of it. Chances are, the gym not only has weights and cardio machines but also some fun classes, a pool, and maybe even a sauna. If you've never been to a gym before, it can be kind of an intimidating place. I know. I used to be afraid of the gym. I always feared that I would break a weight machine or fall on my face while running on the treadmill. If you have similar fears, bring a workout buddy or enlist the help of a trainer to show you the ropes, or find other ways to get your workout in without going to the gym.

If you don't like going to the gym: Go for a bike ride. Kickbox. Practice yoga. Play kickball. Learn self-defense. Join an intramural sports team. Take a hip-hop class. Go rock climbing. Learn a martial art. Play Ultimate Frisbee. Paddleboat. Have a snowball fight. Join a fitness boot camp. Go out dancing. Train for a marathon. Learn to play the drums. Climb trees. Learn to juggle. Kayak. Go surfing. Play capture the flag. Have a water-balloon fight. Walk dogs. Go sledding. Jump on a trampoline. Go hiking. Play dodgeball. Wash cars.

Food (Sort Of)

Cafeteria food isn't exactly the most nutritional dining experience. In many college cafeterias, it's all-you-can-eat, buffet style, so you can go for seconds and thirds and fourths. There are no limits, and sometimes it's tempting to take advantage of the lack of boundaries, even if the food is unappetizing. The cafeteria is often such a social place that you may find yourself spending up to two hours there hanging out with friends. In those two hours, you might not even realize that you've already inhaled four cups of frozen yogurt. Watch what and how much you eat—take stock of all your options, and then make healthy choices.

Stop the "fat talk." Don't call yourself or others "fat" or otherwise engage in any negative talk about your or other people's weight, physical appearance, or eating habits. These types of conversations are toxic for everyone involved and only perpetuate negative body image issues. Love yourself and your body, and help others to do the same for themselves.

Purchase a meal plan that suits your lifestyle. Most schools have a few different options for meal plans, so try to choose one that works best for you. A meal plan is usually some combination of a certain number of cafeteria meals per week and a certain amount of "flex dollars" to be used at other cafés and eateries on campus. Find out whether your cafeteria is open all day or you're required to eat your meals at designated times during the day. If you think you might have trouble sticking to a restricted meal schedule, buy a plan with fewer meals and more flex dollars, or nix the flex dollars and cook some of your meals in the dormitory kitchen. Cooking is always a better option if you know how, have the time, and use healthy ingredients. But if you'd rather not have to think too much about food, opt for a meal plan that allows you three dining-hall meals a day—and get what you paid for by sticking to it.

Limit those take-out orders. Dining-hall food may not be the ideal gastronomic experience, but neither is pizza or Chinese takeout. Only go out to eat or order in on special occasions, on the weekends, or when you are cramming and desperate for a study break.

> *I became a vegetarian three weeks before I went off to college. It was so hard to do! I lasted about a year and a half, but I don't recommend it unless you have been a vegetarian for a very long time and know what you're doing. There was very little in the way of healthy food at my college, not to mention healthy vegetarian food. I would sometimes eat chicken if I was sick and felt the need for protein, but being a vegetarian ran me down because I was depriving myself of essential nutrients and eating things that didn't replace what my body needed. I'm back to being an omnivore now, at least until I'm out of college and can better control what I'm eating. It's so much more practical!*
>
> *— Carolyn Spalding, Lafayette College*

Make the most of the dining-hall experience—take food to go!
Even if you show up at the dining hall right before it closes, it's likely you'll be up late enough to have a second dinner or at least a late-night snack. Take food from the dining hall. Some cafeterias even have a "lunchbox" option, in which your meal plan includes to-go meals. If you grab something to munch on later that's moderately healthy, you will be less likely to order pizza when the craving for a second dinner arises.

Or maybe you know you won't be up in time for tomorrow's dining-hall breakfast, so go ahead and grab a bagel, some cream cheese, and a cup of orange juice.

Make healthy food choices. When you can eat pretty much anything you want thanks to buffet-style cafeteria dining, you may find it hard to resist eating French fries and frozen yogurt at every meal. Not to mention that you're so busy with your classes and your social life that the last thing on your mind is monitoring the nutritional value of your food. So I'll keep it simple for you. Follow these easy tips for making healthy food choices in the dining hall:

1. *Use a small plate.* Trick yourself into thinking you're eating more than you actually are.
2. *Eat only when you're hungry and stop eating when you're full.* Believe it or not, your body often knows better than you do when it needs some fuel or it's had enough. Listen to it.
3. *Choose real, whole foods over processed foods.* Processed foods are foods that have been significantly altered from their natural state—typically canned, frozen, or prepackaged. Opt for natural foods.
4. *Eat something raw and fresh with every meal and snack.* Have an apple at breakfast, some raw almonds for a midmorning snack, carrots with your sandwich at lunch, blueberries and yogurt for an afternoon snack, and salad with dinner.
5. *Opt for whole grain instead of white.* This means for pasta, bread, and rice.
6. *Drink water with your meals instead of soda or juice.* You can never have enough water throughout the day, and soda and juice can be a huge source of unnecessary sugar.
7. *Limit your fat and sugar intake.* Goodness knows we love our frozen yogurt and chocolate chip cookies, but try to limit yourself to one cookie or one small cup of fro-yo per day. Oh, and lay off the creamy salad dressing—opt for olive oil and balsamic vinegar instead.

Always remember: a little bit of weight gain is not the end of the world. College is a time of transition and major changes to your lifestyle. It's only natural that your body changes, too. Don't obsess over it—instead, give your body time to adjust and make healthy eating a priority.

> *My senior year of high school, I lost twenty-five pounds of extra weight through healthy eating and exercise. Still, I was extremely self-conscious about my body when I got to college. The pressures of the new environment caught up with me in the spring, and I started exercising more and eating less. I lost fifteen pounds and loved that suddenly people were noticing me. Diet and exercise quickly became an obsession. I became addicted to weighing myself, watching the numbers on the scale sink lower and lower. During the two weeks of finals, I dropped another fifteen pounds and returned home for the summer skeletal thin. The last two years have been a long process of growth and recovery, but that summer and the next fall are awful memories to me now. People close to me have since admitted that they were worried about me but didn't know how to approach me—but I know now that I would have been grateful for their intervention.*
>
> *— Hannah Rochau, Yale University*

If you or someone you know starts to become obsessive when it comes to food, get help. College is such a stressful environment, and it's also one that encourages you to reinvent yourself. Fear of the freshman fifteen on top of unrealistic images of women's bodies in the media pressure young people to pursue an impossible physical ideal. For this reason, many college women develop eating disorders, such as anorexia and bulimia. They respond to the pressures and fears by either not eating at all or by binge eating and purging their food, thereby endangering their health. If you or any of your friends show signs of an eating disorder, talk to a counselor immediately or contact the National Eating Disorder Association (NationalEatingDisorders.org) helpline at 1-800-931-2237.

Stress: Your Biggest Enemy and Your Most Loyal Companion

In college it will seem like no matter what you get done or how few commitments you make, there will always be something to stress about. Whether it's midterms, papers, sports practices, relationships, phone bills, or rehearsals, something will always be looming over your head. And as these things continue to hover over you, your stress level may rise to meet them, often putting you in overdrive and pushing your body into a state of anxiety. When you find yourself fighting headaches, muscle tension, insomnia, acne, or nausea, believe it or not, you could be stressed out. So listen to your body—it's probably trying to tell you something.

Remember there are some things you can't control, and there are some things you can't change. Learn to accept that certain things are out of your reach, so there's no point in stressing about them. You're better off keeping focused on the things you can control and change.

A healthy body yields a healthy mind: make sure you are exercising regularly and eating healthily. The best way to prevent and manage stress is to exercise and have a well-balanced diet. Make sure you are always eating a ton of fresh and whole foods, and hit the gym when you feel overwhelmed. Exercise is an incredible way of releasing stress. The more you do it, the better you will sleep, the better you can concentrate, the better you will look, and the better you will feel— making you well equipped to handle stress.

Set aside time for relaxation. Time for yourself in a stress-free context is just as important as time for classes, studying, a social life, activities, or whatever other commitments you have. Make a point to schedule time for you and only you—whether it's to give yourself a facial, read a few chapters of the newest vampire novel, or just paint your toenails. Do whatever you can engross yourself in without thinking about anything else but the activity before you.

Talk to a counselor or therapist. Every college's student health center has mental-health services that are free and available to all its students. Use them. Think about it: outside the college context, people shell out as much as $150 for one session with a therapist (or counselor—they are synonymous). Now there can be a stigma attached to therapy, I know, but it doesn't deserve such a bad rap. Therapy isn't "just for crazy people." It's for anyone who could use someone to talk to—about anything and everything. For all you know, you have all the answers yourself—but you won't dig them out unless you talk through your concerns with an attentive, unbiased listener. So don't be afraid to open up to a counselor about whatever is bothering you. Think of that hour a week as "me time"—time that you are taking out to focus on yourself and your mental health, just like you do for your physical health when you go to the gym. The feelings that cause stress tend to fester inside you. It's best to let them out, whether it's through exercise or through talking them out.

Keep your perspective. It might feel like the world is crashing down around you, but stop and think to yourself, "Will this matter a year from now?" If the answer is no, let it go. Figure out what's really worth your mental energy, and focus on that.

Be honest with yourself about how much you can put on your plate. Yes, college opens up a lot of doors, and there are activities you can participate in that you didn't even know existed. It's tempting to try to have your hands in everything, but the fact is, you won't be able to do it all. Don't spread yourself thin. Be realistic about what you can fit into your schedule and about what you can expect from yourself. Besides, it's better to be an enthusiastic and dedicated member of a few clubs than a scatterbrained, distracted member of more organizations than you can count on your fingers and toes.

Don't procrastinate. The more you put things off, the longer you worry about getting them done. Just accomplish whatever you can as soon as you have the time to do something.

If you are feeling overwhelmed, break it all down. What will stress you out the most in college is figuring out how to accomplish all the things you have to do in such a short period of time. You might find that you are so apprehensive about the magnitude of what you have to accomplish that you just stop and give up. Break it down. Make a list of all the things that are stressing you out; then make a plan that involves managing each problem separately. You may find that what you thought were huge, unmanageable problems are really just a series of smaller, manageable tasks. If this isn't the case, you've overextended yourself. Drop one or two of the ten organizations you are part of or audition for just one play instead of two.

Write things down. The less you have to remember on your own, the more relaxed your mind will be. Make sure your planner or calendar is up-to-date with all your exams, due dates, appointments, rehearsals, practices, and meetings. Always keep a small pen and notebook handy wherever you go, so if you remember something while you're walking down the street or eating in the dining hall, you can jot it down before you forget.

If you start to feel so stressed out that you are having trouble functioning, get help. Stress has a habit of building up, especially if it's not dealt with. Oftentimes the stress ends when the day ends, and as soon as another day begins, you are stress free. But if you find that your stress has magnified into anxiety (your hands get clammy, your chest gets tight, you can't sleep, and/or you have trouble breathing) or you feel sad and empty all the time, you need to see a doctor or counselor immediately.

Dealing with depression. Depression is more likely to appear in women than in men, and it is also disturbingly common among college students. Therefore, as college women, we are especially at risk of becoming depressed, whether it is caused by relationship problems, a breakup, family issues, stress, or adjusting to the new environment. We all feel down sometimes, and we all have our good days and our bad days. But if your bad days have stretched into bad weeks or months, you may be clinically depressed. If you or someone you know is suffering from any of the following symptoms, consider seeking help: loss of or increased appetite; loss of interest, pleasure, energy, or motivation; continual feelings of sadness; withdrawal; insomnia or sleeping too much; lack of concentration; feelings of helplessness, hopelessness, and worthlessness; excessive crying; irritability; thoughts of suicide or suicide attempts.

My first semester was a struggle in many of the typical ways—academics were competitive, I hated my major, and I was far from home. However, it was also challenging in another way: I had undiagnosed depression. All around me, my peers seemed to be adjusting easily to their new lives, while all I wanted to do was lock myself in my room and cry. I didn't know why I was so sad, but I felt something was wrong with me. I was afraid and ashamed to ask for help, but through the intervention of loved ones, I began therapy and eventually went on antidepressants. Two years later, I'm no longer on meds, and although I still have bad days, I consider myself a generally happy person. I only wish I'd sought help sooner, because I feel like I missed out on a lot in my first two years.

— Hannah Rochau, Yale University

If you think you or someone you know is suffering from depression, particularly if you or that person is having suicidal thoughts, talk to a counselor or doctor right away or call the Mental Health America (NMHA.org) crisis hotline at 800-273-TALK.

CHAPTER SIX

GETTING SOCIAL: MEETING PEOPLE AND HAVING FUN

Thank goodness for the weekend. Friday night (or better yet, Thursday night, if you've scheduled your classes accordingly) signals the start of the weekend, which means it's time to lay those books to rest and let the games begin. It doesn't matter when you choose to free your mind of calculus and Shakespeare, just as long as you do. You need to give yourself some time for the other very important half of college life: meeting people and having fun. True, it's quite important that you make friends with your textbooks and even better friends with your professors, but I guarantee you'll have a lot more fun with your fellow students. You no longer have the security blanket of your high school clique to help you feel socially safe come Friday night, so now you've got to find a new posse. The great thing about college is it's filled with people who are just as excited and bewildered as you are to be here. You've just got to meet them all, and then from there, you'll find people to hang out with on the weekends or in your downtime during the week. Fortunately for you, college is filled with a variety of opportunities to meet and get to know people, whether it's through organizations, events, or parties.

Meeting People

Let me say this first and foremost: you WILL make friends, I promise. The idea of making a whole set of new friends in this new college environment can be intimidating, I know—especially if you went to a small high school, have lived in the same town all your life, and haven't had to make new friends since kindergarten. On the other hand, maybe you've moved around quite a bit growing up, so by now you're fairly adept at making new friends wherever you go. Whatever the case, when you get to college, everyone else will be going through the same transition you are—so they want to meet you just as much as you want to meet them. The most important thing is to not put pressure on yourself. Be open to everyone you meet, and focus on how exciting it is to be in a new place where you'll get to know and learn from so many new people, each with his or her own unique experiences.

Get a head start over the summer by meeting classmates from your hometown or participating in preorientation programs. Chances are, you can find out from your school if any of your classmates are from your hometown. Get in touch with them, whether it's through Facebook or some other means, and arrange to meet over coffee or lunch. Having that common ground could be a good foundation for a friendship, and at the very least, you'll feel more comfortable starting school knowing at least one or two of your classmates already. Also, as I mentioned in Chapter 1, many colleges offer programs for incoming freshmen during the summer that are intended to facilitate bonding with your classmates.

Meeting people through Facebook: Although it may be tempting to log on to Facebook and send and accept friend requests to any and all future classmates that you haven't even met yet, resist the temptation! While Facebook is definitely a great way to connect with people, it's a good idea not to befriend someone on Facebook until you have actually met them in person. To get in touch with your classmates, try joining your class's Facebook group first; then add new friends as you meet them.

Keep an open mind with everyone you meet—and don't judge. Everyone is different—with his or her own unique history, culture, background, and experiences. Countless factors shape who a person is, so no single factor defines any one person. Keep this in mind as you meet new people. Perhaps where you come from everyone looked similar, dressed similarly, practiced the same religion, shopped at the same stores, and held the same beliefs. But when you go off to college, this won't be the case, so it's important that you are open and accepting of everyone you encounter. Lay those stereotypes and biases aside, and get to know each person as a unique individual whom you will inevitably learn from, just as each person will learn from you in turn. If you ask me, this is the most enriching part of the college experience.

Seek out cultural and racial diversity. If you grew up in a town that is racially or culturally homogeneous, when you get to college, embrace the opportunity to get to know students of cultural and racial backgrounds different from your own. Get to know other cultures, and share your own with other people. You'll be amazed at how much you will discover about yourself in the process of learning about other people.

Start off with what you're interested in. Every college has a myriad of organizations that cater to everyone's different interests. And if an organization doesn't exist for something you are interested in, you can always start one. Your school likely hosts an activities fair for incoming freshmen to introduce you to many of these organizations. If not, peruse your school's website to see if there's a list of clubs and organizations, along with a description of each and maybe an e-mail address for the group's student leader. When you see something that sparks your interest, take the initiative and send an e-mail, telling the person of your interest in possibly becoming a member. Joining an organization is the best way to meet people who have similar interests as you.

Here are some ideas for the kinds of organizations you might consider joining:

▷ **Student government or dorm council.** This is a great way to meet people and get involved in your school and dorm. Plus, you'll get to share your and your classmates' ideas on changes that need to happen at your school—and take part in making those changes happen!

▷ **Sport or athletic activity.** This could be a varsity sport or a club or intramural sport. Be aware that varsity sports take up lots of time and are for those who take the sport very seriously, whereas club or intramural sports tend to be more laid-back and just for fun.

> *Freshman year I decided to join my university's Division I women's rowing team to stay in shape, try something different, and meet new people. This was honestly one of the best decisions I ever made. This challenging experience facilitated a lot of personal growth. We practiced at 5:30 or 6:30 a.m. almost every day, even during the off-season, plus lifted weights three days a week in the afternoons. Needless to say, my schedule differed from my nonathlete friends. Juggling practice, socializing, and schoolwork definitely took some work, but as a result, I became so much more efficient. The hardest part was forming solid bonds with my friends who did not row. They started their study parties during the week about the time I felt ready for bed. On the weekends I was either exhausted from the week or had a race. I remedied this by living with my nonrower friends sophomore year so we could spend more downtime together, which also provided a welcome reprieve from the drama of the team.*
>
> *— Diane, Creighton University*

▷ **Admissions or orientation program.** Many schools need current students to help usher in incoming classes by giving tours of campus, facilitating new-student-orientation programs, or providing support or mentorship to new students. You'll learn about and share what excites you about your school, as well as meet fellow students.

▷ **Community service organization.** These types of organizations do everything from serving at soup kitchens to tutoring elementary school students to building homes. There's no better way to meet and make friends than while working in service of others.

▷ **Newspaper, literary magazine, science magazine, or any other publication.** If you're interested in writing, write for a publication. Or perhaps you want to be a photographer, a layout designer, a copyeditor, or even a business manager. All school publications need students to fill these roles. If none of the existing publications appeal to you, start your own publication about whatever you want. The possibilities are endless.

> *During orientation, my counselor told me that the best way to make a large school feel small was by meeting people. I knew that it would be easier to meet people if I joined an organization or participated in an internship. In high school, I was avidly involved in the school newspaper, so when I saw that my college's newspaper was hosting a recruitment meeting, I made sure to attend. At the meeting, inquiring students were separated into groups, depending on their particular interests, and asked to submit an application and pass a test. After a semester of interning for free as a designer, I was offered a paying job in another department! Not only had I met people by pursuing something I was truly interested in, but I'd also turned the experience into a lucrative opportunity.*
>
> — *Ashley Villanueva, University of California, Berkeley*

▷ **School television or radio station.** This is your chance to get recognized on campus, whether it's by name, face, or voice.

▷ **Sociopolitical organization or advocacy group.** Whether you feel strongly enough about your political affiliation to join the Young Republicans or Young Democrats or you want to advocate for environmental causes or women's rights, you will find a group with like-minded students in these types of organizations.

▷ **Choir, glee club, orchestra, band.** If music is your passion, continue with it through college. You will be among others with such talents, and you'll find that music is taken much more seriously and you'll learn much more.

▷ **Drama or dance club, a cappella or comedy group, play or musical.** If you like to perform, there are countless opportunities for you. Even if you have never been in a play, try out anyway if you're curious about it—you never know! Or try working behind the scenes, maybe on lights or sound or as a costume designer or makeup artist.

▷ **Department, major, or industry club or association.** Joining a club or an association related to your intended major or career aspiration is an excellent way to build a network that could come in handy even years after you've graduated college. It's never too early to start making those career connections.

▷ **Religious organization.** Most colleges have student-run religious organizations that sponsor organized activities and provide a site where you can meet new people with similar religious backgrounds.

▷ **Cultural group.** College is a great place to meet people of your same culture, race, or ethnicity. A cultural group on campus is a good place to start learning about yourself, as well.

▷ **Research lab.** If you are planning on pursuing a career in the sciences, joining a research lab in your department is a great way to gain research experience while meeting others with similar interests. Doing research in a lab is also important experience to have if you eventually decide to pursue a higher degree—especially a doctorate.

▷ **Sorority or co-ed fraternity.** At many colleges, the entire social arena is dominated by Greek life. If your college is one of them, and you're into being well-informed of all the social happenings every weekend, joining a sorority or co-ed fraternity just might be for you.

"Going Greek," or joining a sorority, was probably the best decision I've made so far in college. For the past two years I have been commuting to college from home and have felt the difficulty of creating friendships. I would go to class and simply leave right after, not sticking around and not even being aware of events that were going on. Becoming Greek helped me forge new friendships, especially through social events that allowed me to interact with people who share my interests. The best part of my organization is that it matches two of my core values: community service and academic excellence. I thus hold the utmost respect for my organization and take pride in being a part of it!

— Jennifer Conde, University of South Florida

Join whatever sparks your interest, but don't spread yourself thin. I've touched on this before, but it's important to mention it again. As soon as you get to college, you might have aspirations to join ten different organizations that all seem equally exciting to you. Remember, you have four whole years to try out everything you can. Although there's no harm in signing up for all the clubs that sound fun to you at first, there's no need to cram everything into your first semester—or first year, for that matter. As soon as you see you can't physically attend all the meetings for thirteen different clubs and organizations, don't feel guilty about reducing your commitments. Most college students can only handle one to four extracurricular activities and still do well in their classes, have a social life—and get enough sleep! Be honest with yourself about how much you can handle.

You don't need to join an organization to make friends in college. Eat in the cafeteria and strike up some conversations. Study at the library. Attend group-study sessions. Keep that door open to your dorm room. Throw parties. Go out to dinner with a work colleague. Talk to the guy who sits next to you in class. Go to parties hosted by organizations. Hang out on the quad. Host a movie night. Meet your roommate's friends. Go out dancing. Participate in new-student-orientation activities.

At the same time, if you do join an organization, don't let it consume all your time. It's easy to let your membership in an organization take precedence over the rest of your life, especially if you're really into it and you hold some kind of position of authority. There's nothing wrong with dedicating yourself to anything, just as long as it doesn't become too stressful and it's still a fun part of your life. Don't let your grades fall, your health regress, and your stress level increase because of your commitment to an organization. Remember, too, that you don't have to do anything just to please other people. It's important that you try new things, but also know it's okay not to follow through if you realize the commitment is just too much for you.

The Party Scene

Parties are probably what you are looking forward to the most, and justifiably so. College parties can be fun and crazy, no doubt, or they can also be relaxing and chill. But the one thing you can't avoid when it comes to partying is the presence of alcohol. It's important to mention that alcohol is illegal for those under twenty-one. It is a dangerous drug that impairs judgment and can damage your body. It is also a huge part of college life, so I will treat it as such in this chapter. It's important that you make your own decisions about alcohol. It is a part of college life in general, but it doesn't have to be a significant part of *your* life. No matter what you decide, you'll have fun regardless. It's virtually impossible not to have a blast in college.

It's amazing how many different ways and reasons college students have to celebrate. Here's a little preview of the types of parties you might encounter during these next four years. And if you don't encounter any of these, then that might be just enough incentive to throw a party yourself.

▷ **Pregaming.** Usually hosted in a dorm room, it's a party before you hit an actual party. This party provides a site for everyone in your crew to meet people before hitting the scene. It's usually small and intimate and includes cocktails or drinks of some sort. This eliminates the hassle of fighting the masses at the real party for something to drink. It's a great way to start the night. In some rare cases, pregaming could turn into a full-on party.

▷ **Frat or sorority party.** Since they are hosted at fraternity or sorority houses, these parties often have a ton of room for dancing and games. If Greek life dominates at your school, these parties get crowded. So if you drink, you'll probably spend most of your time pushing your way to the keg and then waiting with an empty cup until the keg master chooses to fill it up. Also, you will most likely get spilled on. Wear shoes that can handle beer spillage.

▷ **Dance party.** If you ask me, these parties are the most fun because they aren't centered around alcohol—and who doesn't love to dance? They may be hosted by a fraternity or sorority, a club or organization, or simply roommates who have a big dorm room and good music to dance to. There might even be a real DJ or at the very least a great playlist.

▷ **Tailgating.** These parties are centered around sports events, such as football games. Students (and often alumni and local fans) get together for some food and beer to get excited before the game, but you don't have to be a sports fan to attend or enjoy the tailgate. Show some support for your team, though, if you feel moved to. These parties are the college version of high school pep rallies, but without all the cheesiness.

▷ **Drinking games.** Card games, beer pong, flip cup, you name it. These can be fun and ridiculous, but they can also be an incredibly stupid way for people to drink in ways that are out of their control. Know your limits. Players of drinking games often have no mercy for lightweights. Never drink more than you want to, and never let a jerk in a baseball cap tell you "the rules" say you have to take another drink.

▷ **Formal or semiformal.** Not only do fraternities and sororities host formal or semiformal dances and balls, but these types of events are also sponsored by clubs, organizations, and even the school itself. Look forward to a fancy night of food, cocktails, and dancing—and don't forget to take some pictures!

▷ **Mixer.** Often hosted by fraternities and sororities, mixers are hosted to get people acquainted with one another and usually "mix" together members of two or more different groups.

▷ **Theme party.** These parties dominate in college because there are so many possibilities. They usually require guests to dress up in some sort of costume, and the music, decor, food, and drinks always correspond to the theme.

Typical College Theme Parties

▷ **ABC (Anything But Clothes).** No clothes allowed, but this doesn't necessarily mean naked. Think: trash bags, boxes, duct tape, towels, coconuts, lampshades... whatever works!

▷ **Around the world.** This party is usually a team effort by several different dorm rooms. Each room represents a different country, with corresponding decorations, drinks, and food.

▷ **Rubik's Cube.** Everyone wears six articles of clothing, each matching one of the colors found on a Rubik's Cube: red, orange, yellow, green, blue, and white. Throughout the night, trade articles of clothing with other guests, until you are wearing one solid color.

▷ **Stoplight.** Wear green to show you are available, yellow to say "It's complicated," and red for "Hands off, I'm taken."

▷ **Graffiti.** Also called a "highlighter" or "black light" party. All guests wear white T-shirts and are given highlighters to write messages on one another's shirts—and the messages can only be seen under the black light. Make the most of the black light by decorating the room with white objects, putting neon food coloring in the beer cups, and handing out glow sticks.

▷ **Letter.** Pick a letter of the alphabet to dictate the theme for the night, and guests just need to dress as anything starting with that letter. So with the letter P, you could dress as a pirate, Paris Hilton, a penguin, or a paperboy.

▷ **Too small.** Everything you wear should be too small, or you should be too small for everything you wear. Let's not forget that everything else should be too small—the cups for the drinks and maybe even the room for the party itself.

▷ **Heaven and hell.** This party works great if the locale has two levels. Heaven on the first floor, with white decor and fruity drinks, and hell in the basement with dark decor and fiery drinks. Guests, of course, dress as angels or devils.

▷ **Toga.** This tribute to ancient Greece is actually just an excuse to show a little bit of skin. Be original and don't use a plain white sheet. Use bright colors instead. And try dressing up your costume with a gold belt and a laurel crown.

▷ **Hawaiian luau.** Yup, another excuse to bare as much as possible and a good time to sport your sexy bikini top. Accessorize with flowers in your hair and a lei around your neck.

▷ **Decade.** Baggy jeans and flannels for the '90s, off-the-shoulder tees and side ponytails for the '80s, bellbottoms for the '60s... you get the idea. And the music should be appropriate for the decade as well!

▷ **Color.** All guests must dress in the color chosen by the host, while the host provides decor, food, and drink of that color as well.

▷ **Movie theme.** Pick a movie, dress like the characters, play the movie soundtrack, drink what the characters drink, eat what they eat, and play the movie during the party, of course.

▷ **And the list goes on:** Pajama. Underwear only. Casino. Halloween. Quarterbacks and cheerleaders. Superhero. Masquerade. Foam. Paint. Cabaret. Famous who? Fantasy. Naughty or nice. Rock stars and groupies. Seven deadly sins. Cross-dress. Dead celebrity. The list is endless!

> *It's important to go all-out when you dress up for a theme party. I once wore shiny blue spandex pants, a neon leotard that had belonged to my mom, and a superhigh ponytail (with a scrunchie, of course!) to an '80s theme party. It's so much more fun if you crank it up a notch! You meet more people, you're automatically interesting, and I've found that I've gotten respect from people I don't even know for taking the theme seriously.*
>
> *— Carolyn Spalding, Lafayette College*

Throwing a party? A few tips to remember:

▷ **Decide on a party type and/or theme.** For example, a dance party with an '80s theme or a mixer with a stoplight theme. Or you don't have to have a theme at all.

▷ **Pick a location.** Make sure it suits the type of party you are throwing—you'll need a ton of room if you're throwing a dance party! For an "Around the World" party, get as many dorm rooms in your building to participate so you'll have as many countries represented as possible.

▷ **Send out a Facebook invite a week or so ahead of time.** A week gives people enough time to buy a costume (if they need to), but not so much time that they forget about the party by the time it happens. Make sure you include a witty description to get people excited!

▷ **Decorate according to the theme (if there is one).** The most memorable parties go all-out when it comes to the theme, so don't slack on this part. If you are throwing a black-light party, make sure your dorm room is filled with decor that will glow under the black light!

▷ **Make some room.** Push furniture to the side and hide all valuables.

▷ **Put out trash cans or recycling bins in visible places.** The more accessible they are, the less cleanup you'll have at the end of the night.

▷ **Post signs for the bathroom.** You don't want a confused partygoer mistaking the potted plant in your bedroom for a urinal.

▷ **Set the mood with lighting.** Lighting can make a huge difference in the mood of the party. If it's too bright, your guests won't feel as relaxed. Dim the lights no matter what kind of party it is, or go all out and get a black light, a strobe light, or a disco ball.

▷ **Make sure you have enough cups and lots of ice.** It's better to buy more than you think you need, because you can always use the extra cups and ice for your next shindig.

▷ **Put together a suitable playlist.** Your playlist should match the theme, if there is one (disco and funk for the '70s, etc.). Make sure the music is upbeat, so you can keep the energy of the party up. If you don't have a playlist, check for music online, pick a danceable Pandora station, or search your favorite music videos.

▷ **Provide refreshments.** Provide some drinks (including nonalcoholic options)—make sure they fit the theme if you have one—and also encourage your guests to bring their own drinks. If your party is on the smaller side—and especially if you have a theme that lends itself to food, like a Hawaiian luau party—it's a good idea to provide some munchies for your guests.

▷ **Have someone play bartender.** If you're just going to have beer, no need to worry about this as much, but if you plan on providing mixed drinks, it's best to have someone man the alcohol.

Handling Your Alcohol

If you choose to drink in college, it's important that you know how to take control of yourself when it comes to alcohol consumption. Drinking can be fun, but it can also be unsafe. Obviously the safest thing to do is not drink at all (and just make fun of everyone else acting stupid while drunk), but if you choose to drink, keep the following things in mind.

I was a pretty big homebody in high school and had never been confronted with the decision of whether or not to drink. So at the first big frat party I went to, I felt like all eyes were on me. I didn't object to others drinking, but I was afraid of getting caught and not knowing my limits. A fellow freshman guessed I was uncomfortable drinking and advised me to just fill my cup with anything. I grabbed the cranberry juice but ended up spilling it in front of one of the junior girls I was trying to impress. As the party filled up, I was convinced that everyone could tell I was a sober loser. Overwhelmed, I shoved my way out the back door. I caught the eye of yet another of those junior girls who came over to ask me what was wrong. I choked out something about not wanting to drink and feeling awkward. She put an arm around me, called the shuttle, and waited with me until it arrived. She assured me that frat parties don't have to be everyone's style and that when she was in my position in her freshman year, it wasn't long before she found friends who didn't care whether or not she drank.

— Erica Irving, Yale University

Know your limits. The general rules are: 1) the smaller you are, the lower your tolerance, 2) the more often you drink, the higher your tolerance becomes, and 3) the less food you have in your stomach, the faster you get drunk. Just get to know yourself and how much you can drink so you can avoid having what you drink come back up. Remember: stop drinking before you start to feel queasy or, better yet, when you're feeling mellow, but not even close to drunk. You don't have to be wasted to have fun. Just be smart about it.

Look out for your friends, and have them look out for you.
Who knows what will happen if you've had too much to drink, so it's
important you have someone lucid around to keep you and your friends
from doing anything stupid or dangerous—not to mention to hold your
hair back when you are hunched over the toilet. And **DON'T DRIVE
DRUNK OR LET ANYONE ELSE DRIVE DRUNK.** Hop on the
campus shuttle or call a cab.

"Beer before liquor, never been sicker; liquor before beer, you're in the
clear." For most people, this saying holds true. For others, it doesn't
mean a thing. In general, it's not a good idea to mix it up, no matter
what the order.

Water, water, everywhere. Water is the best cure for all problems
relating to too much alcohol. Alcohol dehydrates your body, so if you
ever start to feel sick after drinking, you need some hydration. Consider
alternating a glass of water with your drink of choice throughout the
night to prevent dehydration. Drink water right after a night of drinking
and, if you get sick, right after puking. Try to down two full glasses of
water before you hit the sack—and don't chug the water, just sip it. To
settle a queasy stomach you can also try ginger ale, saltine crackers,
antacids, or something starchy, like bread.

Know what you're drinking. We've all heard horror stories
about date-rape drugs being slipped into drinks. Don't let it happen to
you. Never drink something that was just handed to you by someone
you don't trust—even if that person is your date. Pour and mix your
own drinks so you know what goes into them and where they come
from. And refrain from drinking any kind of mystery punch. If you are
sleepy or drowsy, find a friend and go home immediately.

To avoid a hangover, eat some greasy food. Believe it or not,
eating some greasy food can help a hangover. Foods like French fries,
pizza, and potato chips "grease" the lining of your intestines, so the
rate at which your body absorbs alcohol is slowed down.

Know your resources for help in case you need it. Keep phone numbers in your cell phone of an on-campus escort service, your RA, the campus shuttle service, an emergency contact, and the student health center emergency number.

Don't drink if you are on prescription medication. Combining drugs (your medication and the alcohol) could really screw up your system—and might even kill you.

If you are with someone who has had too much to drink—especially if they are to the point of throwing up—GET HELP. If your friend is underage, don't let that stop you from getting help. Staying out of trouble is not the priority, and at the student health center, getting you into trouble is not the priority either. The priority is making sure you or your friend is safe. Horrible as it is to think about, there have been a few widely publicized cases in the last few years of college students dying from alcohol-related accidents. Don't think twice about taking your friend to the hospital—emergency rooms are used to seeing inebriated students, and you might save a life. While you are waiting for help to arrive, make sure your friend stays upright and conscious. If he or she passes out or is in an awkward position, there is a risk of choking. Offer water, and don't leave your friend alone.

Alcohol isn't the only drug you might encounter on your college campus. Some college students also abuse marijuana, cocaine, ecstasy, and shrooms. No good can come out of using any of these drugs, despite how much fun their abusers seem to be having. They are illegal and dangerous, so do yourself a favor and stay away from them. College students are even more likely to use prescription stimulants (especially to stay up all night) including Ritalin, Adderall, and Dexadrine, or prescription painkillers, like Vicodin and Oxycontin, to get high. These drugs are easily accessible because they are available through prescription. Again, there are no benefits to abusing these drugs. If you have been prescribed any of them by a doctor, only use your prescribed amount, and don't share them with anyone else.

CHAPTER SEVEN

SEX AND THE "DATING" SCENE: HOOKUPS, RELATIONSHIPS, AND EVERYTHING IN BETWEEN

Ah, the chapter you've been waiting for. I bet you are pretty much fed up with high school dating by now, and rightfully so. You've probably known most of your classmates since childhood, witnessing all of it—nose picking, pimples, braces, squeaky voices, and other less-than-charming stages of growing up. It's time for a new batch of potential suitors to choose from, and college is the perfect place to find them. Take advantage of this opportunity: at no other point in your life will you be able to sample, in one contained place, the personalities of people from all different walks of life. Many of these people will be just as interested in learning about you as you are in getting to know about them. In these next four years you may very well meet the love of your life!

Some say you will meet your future mate in college, even if it's just in passing. Many college sweethearts end up married soon after graduating, and others who were merely college acquaintances discover years later that they were meant to be together. Have an open mind about everyone you encounter, because even if they don't spark intrigue in you now, they may later. Don't be frenzied in your search for a soul mate, however. After all, the best relationships happen naturally. Instead, just embrace this opportunity to meet as many people as you can, and keep your eyes peeled for that special someone. For all you know, he could be sitting in the back of your Modern Architecture class or throwing a football in the courtyard where you're studying.

First things first: two aspects of college make it a very unique setting for all of its newbie residents—easy access to alcohol and unsupervised exposure to sex. These are the only four years of your life when you will be thrown together with thousands of similarly sexually driven people in a completely new place suffused with constant energy and the thrill of discovery—without parental control! Add to that combination copious amounts of alcohol, which minimizes—or even erases—your inhibitions, and you've got quite an exciting, though potentially precarious, mix. The situation begs to be taken advantage of—and many people do just that. In my years at school, I saw naked classmates running through dorms handing out candy during exam time. I even witnessed some nasty business going on in the library stacks. Sexual energy is everywhere!

Let's be realistic: drinking is fun, and sex is fun, too—especially when you have the freedom to do both as much as you want! The thing is, when you're kind of new at both, you probably don't have a good handle on what your limits are in terms of alcohol (see Chapter 6) and what your boundaries are in terms of sex. Why do I bring up alcohol again in the chapter on sex? Because quite often—too often—when sex is involved, alcohol probably came first. So it's important that you have a good grasp of one so you have the mindset to handle the other.

Depending on which school you go to, college is guy-mania. All the guys you ever thought you would never come across, you do. All the guys you said you would never talk to, you do. In high school, I met guys who wanted to be in relationships, but when college came, things were different. The guy I felt was worthy of being in a relationship with didn't want to be in one. Many guys are not willing or ready to be tied down, and all the girls who want to be should make sure to communicate that early on so as not to waste time with someone who is on a different page. The thing I realized is that when the time is right, a boyfriend will come. While some guys are not ready for relationships, maybe you in turn will come to realize that you're not ready either! You might enjoy the single life more than you thought you did!

— Shanell Simmons, Temple University

Sex

Like I said earlier, sexual energy is everywhere in college. It's pretty tough to avoid it! That doesn't mean actually having sex, because that you can avoid if you choose to, but sex as an issue is inevitable. Even if you choose not to bother with it yourself, you may have to deal with other people who want it from you, or friends who need your support when they are navigating all its accompanying responsibilities and confusions. At the very least, you'll have to consider the possibility of being sexiled by your roommate (see Chapter 3)! So it's important to educate yourself. This means understanding your own attitude toward sex, knowing your boundaries, becoming comfortable with your body, and learning about and using methods of contraception to prevent pregnancy and sexually transmitted infections (STIs).

What is your attitude toward sex, and what are your boundaries? Depending on your experiences and exposure to sex, this could be tough to answer, or it could be very easy. Either way, as sex becomes more and more a part of your life in some shape or form, it's a good idea to understand how you really feel about it, so you can make decisions based on your beliefs. When thinking about your boundaries, consider how far you will go, with whom, and in what situation, so you can avoid feeling vulnerable, uncomfortable, unsafe, or regretful later. When it comes to sex, everyone falls somewhere along a spectrum of emotional involvement. Stereotypically, men fall closer to one extreme—they can have sex without the outcome of emotional attachment: no love, no guilt, no regret. Women, on the other hand, are often assumed to fall closer to the other extreme of the sex-emotion spectrum: we have more of those little impediments called emotions that don't allow us as much guiltless freedom as men seem to have. In other words, with sex come feelings—love, guilt, regret. Although some psychological research supports these stereotypes, it's safe to say that everyone is different, and it's more important to figure out where you fall on this sex-emotion spectrum. To help you explore your attitude and boundaries, try asking yourself the following questions:

1. When do I feel it is okay to have sex (when I am attracted to someone, when I'm with someone I trust, when I'm in a monogamous relationship, when I'm married, etc.)?
2. In my opinion, what is the relationship between love and sex, if any? (Is sex natural, having nothing to do with love, or is sex only for two people who are in love, etc.?)
3. When I think and talk about sex, how am I defining it (touching or handling each other's genitalia, engaging in oral stimulation, vaginal intercourse, anal intercourse, etc.)?
4. When I think and talk about sexual partners, who am I referring to (just men, just women, both women and men, one partner, multiple partners)?
5. Can I separate sex from love? If so, to what extent? (Maybe your answer depends on how far you are willing to go.)
6. How far can I go with someone before I start to develop feelings (kissing, touching, intercourse, etc.)?
7. What kinds of sexual activities make me feel uncomfortable or unsafe (intercourse, fetishes, multiple partners, etc.)?
8. Are there any circumstances in which I would feel regretful or guilty after sex?

It may take a while to be able to answer these questions with certainty, and that's okay. You may not know the answers because you don't know enough about sex in general (who really paid attention in sex ed class anyway?) or because you haven't had enough experience with sex to develop your own beliefs about it. Just keep the above questions in mind as you move through college life and every time you are confronted with a decision having to do with sex. The answers will come with experience. The more self-aware you are about your attitude and boundaries, the better informed your sexual choices will be.

Get to know your body. The more familiar you are with your body, the more comfortable you will be in confronting sex. You may feel kind of strange at first, because traditionally we haven't been encouraged to get to know our bodies. Well, fortunately, times have changed. It's important to take the time to learn about your sexual and reproductive organs and about your menstrual cycle.

> *I have always been the only virgin in my group of friends. So I could never relate to any of the stories they would share, and I couldn't contribute because I don't know what sex feels like. At first it wasn't a huge issue, but as freshman year passed, my friends started making fun of me. It was worse when I was talking to guys. I constantly worried to myself, "Should I tell him?" and "Is he going to stop talking to me now?" And every once in a while a guy would stop talking to me because I was a virgin. I often cried because I just couldn't understand how something so sacred could be such a burden. It's not like I'm waiting for marriage or have never been kissed. I just haven't found someone I'm comfortable with. If you don't feel comfortable with a person, how can you share yourself with them? Too many times I've been there to comfort my friends who balled their eyes out because of guys who didn't call them back after sex. It has been through their experiences that I've learned to love who I am, virgin and all. I now feel confident screaming out to the world, "I'm a twenty-year-old VIRGIN! So what?!"*
>
> — Lizdibier Madera, Syracuse University

Visit your gynecologist once a year. By the time you enter college you should have already had your first gynecological examination. If not, schedule one soon. If you don't already have a gynecologist, ask your mom or another older female you trust to help you find one. Or go to the nearest Planned Parenthood health center. The gynecologist's office is a good place to start getting to know your body, and it's important to visit annually to make sure you are healthy. Become familiar with your reproductive system by watching and understanding what happens during your examination. Your doctor will perform an external and internal pelvic exam, as well as a Pap Smear, which is a screening test for cervical cancer. In addition to this test, you may also ask your doctor to test you for any sexually transmitted infections or for pregnancy. Your doctor will examine your breasts for breast cancer and teach you how to perform a breast self-exam, which you should perform monthly. If you are planning on becoming sexually active or you are already, make sure to also ask your gynecologist about different methods of contraception.

Keep track of your menstrual cycle. The menstrual cycle typically lasts about twenty-eight days, but this can vary depending on many factors, including changes in natural hormone levels (often caused by stress) and the use of hormonal contraceptives. If you aren't already, start recording on a calendar when you get your period—whether it's on your mobile device, your laptop, or your old-fashioned wall calendar. Program your phone to notify you when you should be expecting it. If you're on some form of birth control, keeping track should be pretty easy, since the fixed doses of hormones tend to regulate your menstrual cycle. Once you start monitoring it, you'll know when you can blame acne breakouts or crankiness on PMS, and more importantly, you'll be able to determine more positively whether your period is late and if you should be taking a pregnancy test.

Learn about and use contraception. It's probably been drilled into your head since middle school, but it can never be said enough: if you're going to have sex, do it safely. Use contraception to protect yourself from getting pregnant or contracting sexually transmitted infections. When making a decision on which contraceptive to use, it's important to weigh the advantages and disadvantages of each and to consider your own needs. Most college students tend to use either the condom or the pill (or, for extra protection, both at the same time), as they require minimal in-the-moment hassle and seem to be more appropriate for the college lifestyle. If you choose to take the pill—or any other hormonal contraceptive such as the vaginal ring or patch—keep in mind that you will be altering your hormone levels, which can have side effects. Also, there are many types of pills that adjust different hormones at different dosages, so it might take a while to find the one that is right for you and then for your body to adjust to it. The pill is convenient and highly effective, though, as long as you remember to take it at the same time every day! One more important thing about the pill and other hormonal contraceptives: they help prevent pregnancy only; they do NOT protect against sexually transmitted infections. For protection against STIs, you need to use a barrier method, like a condom.

The condom and the pill are not your only options for contraception. Other possibilities include the female condom, diaphragm, cervical cap, vaginal ring, spermicide, implant, intrauterine device (IUD), and shots. Every method has its strengths and weaknesses based on the needs and lifestyle of whoever is using it. It's best to talk to your doctor about your choices.

In case of an emergency... if you are or plan on being sexually active, make sure you know where to get an emergency contraceptive in the event of a condom breakage or any other malfunction—or in case you were too caught up in the moment (a few drinks too many?) to remember to use any form of protection. Emergency contraceptives, such as Plan B One-Step and Next Choice, basically contain a higher dose of hormones than is found in other birth control pills and can help prevent pregnancy if taken within seventy-two hours after sex. You can get them from your gynecologist, your school's student health center, or your nearest Planned Parenthood. Know ahead of time where to go, because once you realize you need it, you'll want to get it ASAP. Keep in mind that emergency contraceptives are just that—they are to be used *only in the case of an emergency*, not as your regular method of birth control. It's not good for your body to take a large dose of hormones on a regular basis.

Learn about sexually transmitted infections (STIs). Sexually transmitted infections, also called sexually transmitted diseases (STDs), are infections that are transmitted through sexual activity. Examples of STIs include chlamydia, gonorrhea, HPV, and HIV/AIDS. A person can have an STI without showing any symptoms and can transmit it to someone else without even knowing it. Hormonal contraception methods do not protect against STIs. Barrier methods, such as the condom and the diaphragm, do offer some protection, but nothing is 100 percent guaranteed, so be aware of the symptoms of sexually transmitted infections. Once you've gotten to know your body better, you'll be able to tell when something isn't quite right. If anything seems out of the ordinary, see your health professional right away, especially if you experience any of the following symptoms in the genital area: abnormal or smelly discharge, bleeding, blisters, boils, swelling, burning sensations, inflammation, sores, growths, irritations, itches, odors, painful intercourse, pus, rashes, tenderness, urine changes, vaginal yeast infections, or warts. To learn more about specific STIs and their symptoms, talk to a health professional.

Pregnancy. Despite all the available methods of contraception, there is no absolute guarantee that you won't get pregnant, unless you remain abstinent. If you miss a period and suspect you might be pregnant, it may be time to take a test. Anxiety and impatience will, understandably, have you rushing to the twenty-four-hour drugstore for a test you can administer privately as soon as possible. Just don't rely solely on the result of a drugstore test. Go to your gynecologist, your student health center, or a Planned Parenthood, and have the test administered by a doctor or nurse as soon as you can make an appointment. Whatever the results, the doctor or nurse who administers the test will be able to give you more information on your options.

Confronting a possible pregnancy can be very difficult to do on your own. Ask for the support of an older person you trust—someone you would feel comfortable talking with openly about how you feel and what your options are. You don't have to go through it alone.

"Dating"

College is the perfect time and place for dating. Actually, dating in college is quite different from dating in any other environment—so different that it might seem like you aren't dating at all. But believe it or not, as you meet more people and start to hang out with them one-on-one, you ARE dating—though you would probably call it "hanging out." Sure, there may not be an official exchange of phone numbers, a shy phone call asking you out, a nervous greeting at the door with flowers in hand, or an awkward night of dinner and a movie followed by a clumsy kiss at the door. It just doesn't happen that way anymore. More likely than not, you'll meet someone at a party or in class, and then you will encounter each other more and more, until one of you works up the initiative to actually plan these encounters. Eventually you will begin to hang out on a regular basis. Dating—er, I mean, hanging out—sort of occurs without your even knowing it, and if you ask me, that's what's so great about it.

> *As soon as I got to campus, I was on the lookout for possible friends and good-looking guys. One boy in particular was funny and cute. We became friends and then more than friends, until one day we were dating in some vague form. However, it started becoming clear to me that because I spent so much time with him, I didn't know my suitemates very well, and they all spent a lot more time together without me. By "settling down" with one person, I had stopped pushing myself socially. So I made the hard decision to break up with my "pseudo-boyfriend." In hindsight, it is the best decision I could have made. Being single gave me the time to spend with new friends and to focus on academics and extracurriculars. College is a period of change and emotional growth, and I know today that my pseudo-boyfriend and I are very different from when we first met.*
>
> *— Macrina Cooper-White, Yale University*

If you start to become interested in someone, keep these tips in mind:

▷ **Be yourself!** You'll be the most comfortable getting to know the other person if you act naturally. And believe me, no matter who you are trying to be, the real you will always be more attractive to that person than a fake you.

▷ **Be confident.** Don't be too eager, but don't shrink away either. You'll scare the person away by being too clingy, but you have to make some kind of effort. Just casually ask him or her to hang out. You've got nothing to lose.

College is filled with events and activities perfect for a date. Go to a concert or a play. Go on a bike ride. Dance. Watch movies and order pizza. Go to a sports event. Cuddle. Visit a local tourist attraction. Go to a club or bar. Picnic at a local park. Go out for coffee. Throw a ball around. Make out. Play a board game. Talk until sunrise on a rooftop. Go bowling. Visit a museum. Work out together. Play poker or another card game. Compete in trivia night at a local bar. Play one-on-one hoops. Sing karaoke. Go to a campus party. Get some ice cream. Listen to music. Lie on the grass. Rummage through a local thrift store. Cook dinner together. Take a salsa class. Play video games.

▷ **Be laid back.** Remember all you're trying to do is get to know someone, or a few someones for that matter, not find your life partner. (That will happen naturally, remember?) So don't read into things, and don't overanalyze. Just have fun getting to know each other. Things tend to get serious really fast in college, maybe much faster than they should. Go slow.

▷ **Don't overthink it.** The point of dating is to hang out and have fun—no stress, no seriousness, no overthinking. So don't fill your time wondering whether someone likes you, what he is doing, or when he is going to call. If you find yourself spending more mental energy on him than you suspect he is spending on you, he isn't worth it. And if he turns out to be a jerk, he isn't worth it. Remember there are a lot of fish in the sea, so if you've discovered a dud, get over it and move on.

▷ **Go with the flow.** Always be in the moment, and free yourself of expectations. The tough thing about dating in any context is that both people not only need to be compatible, but they also need to be on the same page about what they want. This winning combination is difficult to find, so it's best to approach dating with an open mind and not to expect any relationship to become more than what it is in the moment.

Be in the here and now as you get to know people, instead of focusing on what might, could, or should come next.

The bottom line on "dating": have fun, be open, and don't take things too seriously.

Hookups

In college there exists a particular type of sexual interaction that is most commonly known as the *random hookup*. In this situation, two people theoretically get together for the sole purpose of enjoying some physical interaction, however large or small, with no strings attached. The two involved may be friends, they may be acquaintances, or they may be total strangers. Regardless of the nature of their relationship, the point of the interaction is to get some *play*.

Not surprisingly, these random hookups occur quite often, dominating college culture so much that the idea of dating seems foreign on any campus. Hooking up is just too easy. You've got no one to answer to, and neither of you is looking for anything more than a little bit of pleasure, without the hassle of a relationship.

Seems simple enough, right? Well, it could be simple or it could be complicated, depending on what your boundaries are and where you fall on the sex-emotion spectrum. If you have trouble separating sex from your emotions, random hookups might be difficult for you. Once you get physical with someone, it may be hard for you not to get emotionally attached. There's nothing wrong with that. Our bodies are sacred to us, and once we allow someone to cross that threshold, we can't help but feel as though we deserve more than just physical benefits. If, however, you can keep your emotions out of the picture when it comes to sex, random hookups might be easy for you. There's nothing wrong with that either. Sex is a natural and healthy part of being human, and it can be a beautiful way of learning about yourself, expressing who you are, and loving your body—as long as it's safe and it's between two consenting people. Whether you fit into either of these categories or are somewhere in between, it's important to know your boundaries as you figure out how to handle a hookup.

Always remember that you are in control of your own body. Give yourself and your body the respect you deserve, and expect nothing less from other people. Under no circumstances should you ever feel obligated to go further or faster than you want or to do anything with anyone that makes you feel unsafe or uncomfortable. If you are in a situation that you don't want to be in, get out of it. And if you choose not to participate in the hookup culture, it's okay. The choice is yours.

Date rape. A serious yet common issue on college campuses, date rape occurs when the perpetrator is someone the victim knows—a friend or a date. Often the perpetrator uses a date-rape drug like Rohypnol, which causes the victim to forget events that occurred while they were sedated by the drug. Since this type of violation involves someone the victim thought she could trust, it often becomes difficult for victims to come forward. They feel embarrassed, traumatized, and even ashamed.

If someone has forced you or someone you know to do something you didn't want to do, get help. Tell a counselor or a health practitioner immediately, or call the Rape, Abuse and Incest National Network (RAINN.org) National Sexual Assault hotline at 1-800-656-HOPE.

Let's put things in perspective. Once you've experienced a random hookup, you will likely experience one of the following outcomes:
▷ **Thanks, and see ya never.** You forget about him—no discomfort, no regrets.

If this is your outcome, then you probably fall closer to the "no-emotion" end of the sex-emotion spectrum, which means random hookups yield no negative emotional results for you. So that means you're home free, right? Not so fast. The more comfortable you are with hooking up with anyone, the more often you will do it. The more random people you hook up with, the more at risk you are for pregnancy and STIs, even if you aren't having vaginal intercourse. So if you choose to go this route, always be aware and be safe. There's nothing wrong with sexual experimentation as long as you always use protection and get tested regularly for STIs. Remember, too, that even though you can experiment without getting emotional, you may get involved with people who become emotionally attached to you. So be selective of your partners, and although it's just experimentation, it is also sex, and sex should be taken seriously.

Sex and your reputation. Many college campuses are rife with gossip, so if you're the type who cares about what other people say about you, know that your actions could affect your reputation. Engaging in casual sex on a regular basis could get people talking—or worse, trash talking on gossip websites, like CollegeACB.com (formerly JuicyCampus.com) and CampusGossip.com. If you become a victim of gossip like this, hold your head high and rise above it. People who gossip have nothing better to do with their time, but you certainly do.

▷ **Thanks, and see ya tomorrow?** You are so okay with what you did that you hook up with him again and again. No emotional attachment—just a new, um, "play"-mate.

Now this situation seems ideal because two people are getting the action they want, without the baggage, and the risk of STIs is lower because you are only having sex with one person. This is all provided that both people are on the same page and are equally carefree about casual sex. If not, things could get messy. The fact is that some people find that the more sexually involved they get, the more likely they are to become emotionally attached. If one of you gets attached, while the other doesn't, it's best to stop the regular hookup sessions ASAP to minimize the heartache. Now if the feelings are mutual, this could be a good thing. However, relationships based entirely on sex usually don't last. So if you plan on pursuing a legitimate, serious relationship with a hookup, try to lay off the physical stuff for a while and get to know each other on an emotional and intellectual level—this will create a more stable foundation for your relationship than just a physical connection.

> The February of my freshman year, I had my first serious college hookup. Conditions were prime: a Super Bowl party full of freshmen who didn't all know each other and an endless supply of margaritas. The guy and I actually discussed the situation as we spooned later, and we agreed that this was just a hookup, nothing more. But I'd done things with him I'd never done before, and he made me feel good—both physically and emotionally. In spite of myself, I felt an attachment forming—one that caused me a lot of unnecessary heartache. At the time, I didn't know my boundaries or myself well enough to understand my reaction. I've hooked up since, but with more self-knowledge and a better understanding of what works for me personally. I don't think I'd undo that first hookup if I had the opportunity. It was a steppingstone in my life—an essential learning experience.
>
> — Hannah Rochau, Yale University

▷ **Thanks, now let's be friends.** You like him, but you realize that he would make a great friend and nothing more.

Sometimes after exploring a physical connection, two people discover they connect more on a platonic level and ultimately choose to ditch the sex in exchange for a friendship. In this situation, as with the previous one, it's important that both people are on the same page. That is, if one person just wants to be friends, the other person should want the same thing—nothing more, nothing less. If the platonic feelings are mutual, then by all means pursue a friendship—with both of you agreeing that sex is out of the picture from now on.

Just friends... with benefits? Often in college two friends decide that they want to hook up regularly, without pursuing a relationship. They become *friends with benefits*. This may seem like a good idea at first—after all, you're with someone you trust, without the responsibility and commitment of a relationship. For some, this sort of arrangement works splendidly, provided that they can separate the sex from the friendship. For others, sex complicates things because feelings get involved—ultimately destroying the friendship. If you find yourself in a friends-with-benefits situation, proceed with caution, especially if you plan on staying friends.

▷ **What did I just DO?** You feel uncomfortable with what you did, and you regret it.

It's okay to feel uncomfortable and regretful of a random hookup. In most cases, you probably wouldn't have hooked up if the situation had been different (e.g., if you hadn't done five sake bombs in an hour or alternated between vodka and whiskey all night). Whatever the case, just learn from the experience and realize that you probably just aren't cut out for casual sex. And that's a good thing. It's okay to make mistakes, because making them is how you learn what to do differently the next time. And the fact is that a lot of girls in college make the same mistake. So you're not alone. Talk to your girlfriends (or better yet, an older sister) about it. Tell them how you feel. It will help you understand the experience, and you will feel reassured that you're not the only one.

It's so important to be on the same page as the person you are hooking up with. My first "guy" experience as a freshman taught me this. I started hooking up with a sophomore, but I felt that the situation was more casual than he did. I hooked up with other guys, and he said he was okay with that as long as I came back to him. Then one night at a party he saw me kiss another guy—and he freaked out! He told me he wanted to be my boyfriend, but I didn't want a relationship with him. It was a nightmare because we had so many mutual friends and no one knew how to act around him after that. I felt bad that I hurt him, and I know now that this could have been avoided if we had been more open with each other.

— Carolyn Spalding, Lafayette College

▷ **The pangs of unrequited love.** You start to like him, but he couldn't care less, or vice versa.

Now if after this one hookup, one of you gets attached and the other just wants to move on, someone's heart could get broken. If you're the one who can't get him out of your head—and it's fairly obvious that it was just a one-night stand to him—let go and move on. Besides, the healthiest relationships usually don't begin with a one-night stand. On the other hand, if he's the one who wants to pursue a relationship and you're not interested, just be straight with him from the beginning. Let him down easily and as soon as possible. Breaking hearts is hard, but it's a real and inevitable part of life.

▷ **A romance blossoms.** You start to like him, and he starts to like you, too.

If both of you are sincerely into each other, by all means, let the romance begin. However, as I said above, if you plan on pursuing a legitimate, serious relationship, lay off the physical stuff for a while and let the relationship grow from the more stable foundation of an emotional and intellectual connection. If sex is a major part of the relationship from the start, you're balancing on unsteady ground and the relationship is bound to end sooner rather than later. And, believe me, it won't be a happy ending. The healthiest relationships begin with two people really getting to know and becoming comfortable with each other. Take the time to evaluate whether or not you click well enough to get seriously involved. A serious relationship takes time and energy. It's not worth the effort if you find that you don't even have anything in common other than sex.

The bottom line on hooking up: know and stick to your boundaries, and always be safe.

Getting Serious

Don't look for a serious relationship during your freshman year. Use this year as a time to get to know yourself and other people in this new environment. Get to know the different personalities out there, so you can piece together in your mind the type of person you want to end up with eventually. By keeping an open mind and not committing yourself, while still having fun meeting people, you'll be able to make an educated decision later when the possibility of a relationship arises.

Besides, freshman year is a time of exploration. Freshman year is when you find your niche and discover the people that you will be hanging out with and bonding with for the rest of your years at college. These people will be your family away from home. If you've never been in a serious relationship before, you may not know how to find balance between the relationship and the other, just as important parts of your life. Committing yourself to one person right off the bat could mean that you will have very few people to turn to later.

Remember, the best relationships happen naturally. Don't let the search for a soul mate define your college experience. Just have fun and take care of yourself. Do whatever makes you happy. Surround yourself with people you have fun with. If the opportunity for a relationship somehow arises—great. Go for it. If not, it doesn't matter, because you're having a blast anyway!

———

You know you're in a relationship when you...

▷ leave your things at each other's places, especially your toothbrush and a set of pajamas.

▷ make plans for during the day instead of just for late-night rendezvous.

▷ refer to each other as "we."

▷ sleep in the same bed more than three nights a week.

▷ call each other throughout the day to "check in."

▷ find your typically solo activities, like studying, turn into couple activities.

▷ no longer feel the need to wear makeup or otherwise look nice for the other person.

▷ show up at parties together.

▷ talk about your feelings.

▷ say you're "seeing someone" when you get hit on by someone else.

———

If you do happen to fall into a serious relationship, with luck it will happen later on in college, say your junior year, when you're likely more prepared to get serious. Make sure you know what you're getting into. Relationships are difficult to maintain to begin with, and they are even more so in college. They require a lot of time and emotional energy. In order to make them work, you have to be able to trust and be trusted and you must be willing to communicate.

Going the distance: a word on long-distance relationships. If you have a boyfriend in high school and you are planning on staying together in college, chances are, you will be faced with the challenge of a long-distance relationship. Since college relationships require a lot of time and emotional energy, maintaining a happy, healthy relationship becomes even more difficult when both people are living in two different places. Both of you will have two very different college experiences, and both of you will be changing. To keep the relationship strong, while making the most of your individual college experience:

1. *Talk often, but not too often.* Stay connected, but don't let your phone or Skype time prevent you from embracing your college experience. Go out and have fun, and then give him a call when you get home and tell him all about it!

2. *Visit often, but not too often.* Visit each other often enough so you get to know each other's new friends, but not so much that you miss out on what's happening on campus. And when you are visiting, strike a balance between alone time and time with friends. Let him experience the person you are with your friends, not just the one you are with him.

3. *Welcome changes—in you and in your partner.* College will change both of you, probably in very different ways. Be supportive of any changes you see in him, and expect him to do the same for you. The best way for you to grow together is to allow each other to grow separately, too, and to learn to love the new people you both become.

Let the relationship be just one of the many important parts of your college life. As in love as you might be, don't make him your entire life. As my older sister said to me when I was in a serious relationship in college, "You may be flying high, but don't forget your friends and family. They are the ones who keep you grounded." Maintain a good balance between him and the other people in your life.

Be patient and listen. Relationships are not just based on attraction and infatuation, but also on communicating with, trusting, and understanding each other. This kind of strong connection between two people might take a while to build. Make an effort to listen to him and to understand who he is and what he needs; expect him to do the same for you.

Your happiness should come from yourself, not from him. Don't forget your independence. It's okay to lean on him once in a while, but don't become dependent on him, just as he shouldn't become dependent on you. As my mom says, a relationship should be "a union of strength." You and your boyfriend should be independent, secure, and happy with yourselves as individuals first and foremost, rather than depending on each other for personal happiness and security. If you're confident and feel good about yourself and he feels the same way about himself, your relationship will be more likely to last.

Relationships are tough, so it's okay if you realize that you're not ready. This is a crazy time in your life. You are going through a lot of changes, and you probably still haven't gotten to know yourself well enough to become really comfortable with who you are as an individual. Not only that, you've got to handle classes, think about your career, and learn to take care of yourself all at once. It's hard to do all of that and be a good girlfriend at the same time. If you find that it's just too much to deal with, get out of the relationship. It might be painful, but you'll be doing both of you a favor in the long run. Timing is half of what makes a relationship work. If you really are meant to be, you'll be.

The bottom line on getting serious: let it happen on its own, and if it does, make sure your relationship is a "union of strength" in which you are both independent and you always communicate.

CHAPTER EIGHT

BEING INDEPENDENT: LAUNDRY, MONEY, AND OTHER GROWN-UP STUFF

When you go off to college, you may experience independence for the first time in your life. You'll love the newfound freedom and having control over your possessions, your money, your time, your decisions— yourself. But you will soon see that along with freedom comes responsibility. Part of that responsibility involves becoming self-sufficient by doing little things like making your own doctor's appointments, doing your own laundry, shopping for groceries, cooking, getting organized, and managing your time. It also entails taking small steps toward making a living and creating a career for yourself, which includes earning, managing, and saving money; creating a résumé; applying and interviewing for internships and jobs; and building a network of personal and professional contacts. Ugh—it all sounds so serious and intimidating, but the beauty of college is that it's sort of like practice for the real world. You have these four years ahead of you to become your own person and slowly ease yourself into adulthood. And this chapter is a good place to begin.

In learning to become self-sufficient, start small. Self-sufficiency is just another way of saying you can take care of yourself, rather than depending on other people, like your parents. Some good places to start with being independent are learning to do your own laundry or shop for milk from the grocery store when you've just finished the last carton. The sooner you get comfortable with smaller, practical tasks like these, the easier it will be to handle the larger tasks, and ultimately the pressures of college life.

Laundry

Let's start with something simple. If you already know how to do your laundry, you're much better off than I was when I went off to college. If you were lucky enough to have your parents do your laundry for you up until now, the idea of washing and drying your own clothes might sound like a completely foreign concept. Luckily, you have the entire summer before college to start learning under the supervision of your parents. Laundry is going to be an enormous pain. It's better to learn how to do it before you sacrifice your favorite jeans and tops to trial and error. Maybe your mom has some stain-lifting secrets to share. With luck, by the time you enter freshman year, at the very least you'll know how NOT to turn your white shirts pink.

Laundry basics
Sort 'em:
1. Sort your clothes into dark colors, light colors, and whites. Within each of these categories, separate the delicates, heavily soiled, and towels (and other lint-producing fabrics).
2. Empty pockets, turn jeans inside out (prevents quick fading), and close zippers, snaps, and hooks.
3. Pretreat stains—that is, rub detergent or stain lifter directly on them.
4. READ ALL LABELS and follow the instructions. Don't wash an item that's "dry clean only."

Throw 'em in:
1. Choose the temperature and cycle settings. In general: HOT = whites and heavily soiled clothes; COLD = dark colors and colors that bleed; WARM = everything else. If you're not sure about the temperature for a certain article, read the label. There may also be additional controls to set for what you are washing (delicates, permanent press, etc.) and the size of the load you are washing (extra-large to very small).
2. If possible, turn on the machine to start filling with water.

3. Add detergent (DON'T FORGET! I know a few people who have), following the measuring instructions on the package. You may also want to add liquid fabric softener and/or bleach—again following the instructions on the package.
4. Throw in your clothes. Don't overload the machine; leave room for the clothes to circulate.

Dry 'em:

1. Remove your clothes from the washing machine as soon as they're done so they won't wrinkle.
2. Separate hang-dry clothes from machine-dry clothes.
3. Set your dryer cycle to WARM for normal clothes and HOT for sturdier items like towels.
4. Throw in a fabric softener sheet if you didn't use liquid softener in the wash; turn on the machine and let it whirl.

That covers it. Now doing laundry in college will be a little different from doing laundry at home. For one thing, in college you may have to drag or wheel your laundry down to the basement of your dorm building or to a different building entirely, rather than just taking it down the hall. Also, you'll have to pay for every load (wash AND dry), either using a prepaid card or inserting a bunch of quarters into the machine. Here are a few tips for doing laundry in college:

1. Make sure you can pay before you throw in a load. If your college uses a prepaid card system, keep track of how much money is on your card. Always check the amount before you put in your load so you don't have to leave your clothes behind to run to an ATM. If your school uses machines that require quarters, save all you can in a jar or get a few rolls from the bank so you always have a supply.
2. Stay with your clothes while they are in the washer and dryer if you can. Bring some studying to do. Believe it or not, your clothes could get stolen or at least taken out and thrown on a dirty counter or even worse, the floor. If you can't stay, take note of how long the

cycle will take, and make sure you come back a couple of minutes before it ends. Don't forget to come back on time! Be courteous to other students who may be waiting for the machine to be free.

3. Don't leave your laundry basket or detergent lying around unattended. They could get taken or someone could "borrow" them.

4. Do your laundry when no one else does. During the week and early in the day are good. Weekends tend to be busy.

5. Do your laundry on a regular schedule, if you can. Pick a day and time every week or every other week, and make sure you stick to it. You don't want to open up your top drawer one morning to find that you have no clean underwear!

Cooking

Chances are that you'll be on some kind of meal plan, which means you've paid for a certain number of cafeteria meals per day and per week. (For more on food, see Chapter 5.) But remember, the fact that most of your meals are prepared for you doesn't mean you'll never have to cook. Sometimes you may long for a home-cooked meal. Many college students don't think much of their food options in the cafeteria, so it can't hurt to be able to cook some meals yourself. Perhaps you grew up cooking in the kitchen with your dad, so it already comes naturally to you and you already have a few recipes under your belt. If this isn't the case, though, then take advantage of the summer before college to learn a thing or two from whoever cooks in your home.

Learn five or six simple family recipes—or try out some recipes you find online. If you don't have a natural sense of what ingredients taste good together, following recipes might be easier than experimenting in the kitchen. During your summer before college, learn how to cook some of your favorite meals from your family and friends: first cooking alongside the chef and then creating opportunities to prepare the dishes on your own. Invite your friends over for a meal, say, every couple of weeks, for which you cook them a new dish you've learned—and they bring dessert! As you learn—whether it's from a relative, watching cooking shows on television, perusing cooking websites, or just experimenting in the kitchen on your own—you may discover that you have a knack for mastering flavors or at least that you can make a wicked good omelet!

Organization and Time Management

As you start to take control of your own life, you'll have more and more "stuff" to keep track of. When I say stuff, I mean both actual materials, like important documents, and anything in your life that takes up your time, like appointments and assignments. It's important to start organizing your life so you know where all your materials are and you can use your time wisely and efficiently—keeping to deadlines and remembering appointments.

Create your own filing system of essential documents. Whether you use an actual filing cabinet or prefer to store everything electronically either on a hard drive or network, come up with a system that works for you. Make sure every file has an appropriate label and that all documents are placed in descriptive categories so they are easy to find later. Here are some examples of documents that you might want to file away for safekeeping: birth certificate, social security card, and passport; school transcripts and diplomas; health, dental, and/or car insurance documents; car registration and title information; bank account, credit card, and student loan statements; copies of annual income tax returns; and manuals and warranties for any technology owned.

Develop a procedure for keeping track of your schedule, meeting deadlines, and completing tasks. One of the most difficult things to learn in college and beyond is *time management.* It's a skill that is so commonly troublesome for people that there are countless products, websites, and applications to assist consumers in managing their time. Whatever system you decide to use, make sure it includes a calendar for keeping track of appointments and deadlines, along with reminders of upcoming events and due dates. Many online applications, along with their mobile counterparts, have calendars that you can program to automatically notify you via e-mail, text message, or push notification of anything coming up. Also, utilize some type of to-do list application—which most programs have—so you can monitor all the tasks you need to accomplish. Or, if you prefer, go the old-fashioned route and keep written or typed to-do lists.

Start to get a sense of how you utilize your time. When you get to college, at first it'll feel like you have a ton of free time on your hands. But soon you'll realize that it's not that you have all this free time, but rather that most of your time is totally unscheduled, which means you now have to take charge and figure out how to schedule and use your time wisely. I've mentioned some of the below tips in Chapter 4, but keep them in mind:

1. *Determine how many hours per week are free for schoolwork.* Calculate how much time you spend doing nonstudying activities (class, work, sleeping, eating, etc.). Subtract that number from the total number of hours in a week (168), and that's how much time you have left for studying.

2. *Create a study schedule.* Decide exactly which hours of each day you will set aside for schoolwork. Record your study times on your calendar, so these slots of time are just as static as those slots reserved for class, appointments, and other invariable events.

3. *Record all assignment due dates.* Look over the syllabus for each class and record on your calendar all exam dates and due dates for assignments.

4. *Review your calendar on a weekly basis.* Pick a set time each week, like Sunday evening, to review the week and month ahead.

5. *Prioritize your assignments.* As you begin each week—and even each day—prioritize your assignments based on due date and length of time required for completion.

6. *Break up larger, long-term goals into smaller, short-term tasks.* For example, if you have five weeks to write a fifteen-page paper, outline and research it the first week, spend the next three weeks writing five pages a week, then spend the last week revising it.

7. *Multitask.* Make good use of odds and ends of free time, like riding the campus shuttle or sitting in the waiting room for an appointment, to get some studying done.

8. *Minimize last-minute distractions.* The key to time management is sticking to a schedule. If something comes up like a friend suddenly asking you to go see a movie, discipline yourself to refuse unless you get your scheduled studying done first.

Managing Your Money

Money doesn't grow on trees, they say, and when you're in college, you'll wish it did. For some reason, college students are always low on cash. Perhaps it's because most of us would rather party hard than get a job or we don't know how to manage our money or hmm... because tuition these days seems to cost more than the monetary value of an island in the Pacific, but cash seems to disappear into thin air come the weekend. Whatever the reason, you're going to have to earn some money in college, whether it's just your own spending money or to help pay for tuition. And once you have some earnings, you've got to learn to save it and spend it wisely.

It's incredible how easy it is to blow through money on campus. Food is an enormous expense. It just so happens that the dining-hall menu at my university is disgusting, so I got into the habit of skipping breakfast and picking up a coffee and bagel or muffin on my way to class or ordering a sandwich or sushi for delivery when dinner rolled around. This sort of habit did not last very long because my parents were paying for a full on-campus meal plan that I wasn't using PLUS daily off-campus food. I didn't have access to a kitchen or even a microwave, so this seemed logical to me—but the expense was completely illogical.

— Emily Fiona Weddle, University of Delaware

Determine where your money goes. Use the summer before college and your first month or two in college to track all your expenses. There are great mobile applications and websites that will not only keep track of all your spending based on categories, like entertainment, shopping, and dining, but they will also notify you if a credit-card payment is due or you were charged an overdraft fee. If you don't take advantage of these apps and programs, at least jot down your spending in a notebook and keep all your receipts so you can sit down later and make sense of where your money goes. After a month or two, evaluate your spending and determine where you are spending more than you need to.

Cheap ways to have fun in college. Have a movie night in your dorm room. Sit outside and talk. Walk around campus at night. Go window shopping. Have a makeshift photo shoot. Attend free Greek functions. Go to clubs before they start charging a cover. Host and attend room parties. Explore the city by foot. Go on a bike ride. Host a potluck. Have a clothing swap. Have a game night. Go hiking. Attend on-campus performances. Split entrées at restaurants. Go sledding. Go rock climbing.

Set a budget and stick to it. Here's how:

1. Figure out how much you earn. Your income is your wages (minus taxes) and any other sources of money, such as scholarships, loans, and stipends.
2. Figure out how much you need to spend. Categorize your expenses; for example, household, transportation, clothing, food, entertainment.
3. Determine where you can spend less and adjust your budget accordingly to ensure that your expenses do not exceed your income. Set aside 10 percent for savings first (if you can), then money for fixed expenses, then varying expenses.

If you think you'll have trouble sticking to a budget, try physically separating your money for specific purposes. Set up three separate bank accounts:

▷ **Account #1: Fixed expenses.** This is a checking account to cover any expenses that are the same every month. These could include transportation costs or cell-phone bills. Make sure the correct amount is in that account at the end of the month so when you pay bills you don't get charged overdraft fees. Let this be the only account you have a checkbook for, and if you have a debit card for this account, only use it to make those fixed payments.

▷ **Account #2: Personal expenses.** This is a second checking account for other expenses that tend to vary, like clothing, entertainment, and groceries.

▷ **Account #3: Savings.** Let a certain amount of your paycheck—ideally 10 percent or more—go to this account and never touch it. You can even set up automated transfers through your bank, so at a certain time each month—for example, right after you deposit your paycheck—a certain percentage of it gets transferred to your savings account.

I received my first credit card at eighteen. I was thrilled to finally have one and not have to worry about carrying money around all the time. Soon, though, I was swiping my card so often that I eventually spent more than I could pay back right away. It also didn't help that as a college student my income was not exactly ideal. So I struggled to pay off my credit card and ultimately was late on a couple of payments. As a result my interest rate rose, and it took me longer to pay off the card. Lessons to be learned: If you're not mature enough to handle your finances, don't get a credit card. If you do decide to get one, set rules for yourself. Don't spend more than you can pay off each month and also only use it for true emergencies.

— Jennifer Conde, University of South Florida

Be wary of credit card use! You should definitely have a credit card, because it's important to start building good credit for the future. However, you should only use it in an emergency or if you are making a major purchase that you are certain you will be able to pay off at the end of the month. If you use a credit card more than necessary, you'll start spending money you don't have, and you may accumulate a huge credit-card debt without even realizing it—not to mention the interest fees you'll be paying. Keep in mind that if you have loans covering your tuition, you're already going to be in the hole when you graduate—there's no reason to dig yourself deeper! If you know you don't have self-control, don't carry the credit card around with you. Instead keep it locked away for those well-thought-out, necessary, major purchases that you will pay off quickly.

Getting a Job in College

"Is she nuts?" you think to yourself. "How on earth am I supposed to find time to work on top of classes, studying, friends, partying, extracurriculars, working out, dating, and not to mention eating and sleeping?" Believe it or not, it's possible. It depends on how much of a priority money is to you, and chances are, it's a *major* priority, so it might be worth dropping an extracurricular activity or two. Fortunately, college campuses are filled with jobs that you'll be able to fit into your schedule one way or another. For some students, getting a job simply means wasting less time, because they know they otherwise wouldn't be doing anything useful. But there are much better reasons for getting a job in college: you learn important skills like leadership and time management, you learn about potential career paths, you begin to build a network of connections and your résumé, and you learn the importance of making a living.

Work on campus. If your financial-aid package includes a work-study component—which means your financial need qualifies you to work part-time for your school to help pay for expenses—you will definitely have to find a job on campus. If you don't qualify for work study, on-campus jobs are still available to you, but you just won't get priority. On-campus jobs tend to allow more flexibility for your busy schedule. Also, these jobs often pay much better than similar jobs off campus. Your employers are more understanding of the fact that you are a college student and have five hundred other things to make time for. You may be able to make your own hours, and if you need to miss work to finish up a term paper, it will probably be okay as long as you call in. Your boss will most likely recognize that you are a student before everything else, so he or she will let you off the hook for academic reasons. These on-campus jobs are often in high demand because of their convenience and flexibility, so start perusing on-campus job postings on your school's website over the summer. The sooner you apply, the more likely you'll be able to snag the job.

Some typical on-campus jobs and places to work: Fitness center. School newspaper. Food services. Admissions office. Office assistant. Campus tour guide. Research assistant. Bookstore. Peer advisor. Community service coordinator. Lab assistant. Library. Alumni relations. IT assistant. Resident advisor. Usher. Tutor. Writing assistant. Orientation leader. Career services.

On the other hand, working off campus might be better for you if you want to get away. Some students prefer off-campus jobs because it's a way of escaping the college grounds for a little while. They are a great way to meet people from the area who don't attend your college and to become familiar with the world outside your campus. The downside is that your employer may not have mercy on you if you've got three papers to write on a weekend that he has you working double shifts on, *both* days. To him, you're an employee first and a student second.

Some typical off-campus jobs. Retail salesperson. Restaurant server. Grocery store cashier. Restaurant hostess. Cashier. Customer service representative. Tutor. Babysitter. Lifeguard. Caterer. Childcare worker. Barista. Bartender.

When you're on the job search, consider how many hours you want to work and when. It's important to have a set idea of how many hours you want to work per week (most college students work an average of five to ten hours per week at an on-campus job). Then decide whether you want to work during the day or on evenings and weekends. Make sure your hours fit around your class schedule. Most offices are only open Monday through Friday, nine to five. With classes and other activities, if you find it hard to put in hours during the day, there are on-campus jobs available where you can work evenings and weekends; for example, at a library, a computer lab, or a cafeteria. Or if you choose to work off-campus, you can babysit, wait tables, or work in retail.

Keep an eye out for temporary ways of making money. Often schools hire students for short-term jobs, like working at a sporting event or a festival. Or some departments, like psychology, even offer payment for participating in studies—which usually just involve filling out a survey.

Accept that you might not be working the most fun or glamorous job in the world. In fact, you might just be doing grunt work, like making copies, filing, sorting mail, and answering phones. These may not be the most exciting tasks in the world, but just take comfort in the fact that those measly chores are putting money in your pocket. Some jobs, like those at the library, pay you by the hour to sit at a desk and study while you wait for the phone to ring or for someone to check out a book.

A few ways to save your money in college:

▷ **Make the most of your meal plan.** I've already mentioned this in Chapter 5, but it's worth reiterating. Since you're paying for it, make sure to use your meal plan instead of spending money at the local diner or ordering pizza. Maximize your dining dollars by always taking food on-the-go with you.

▷ **Don't buy new textbooks.** As I mentioned in Chapter 4, buy them used or online at discount websites, rent them, or buy the e-book version (if there is one—it is always cheaper). If you're really trying to save, share a textbook among a few of your classmates, borrow one from someone who has already taken the class, or check it out from the school's library.

> *My first semester, I spent over $400 on books. My second semester, I spent less than $100. I saved money by asking upperclassmen friends if I could borrow or buy their books from them cheap, and I also searched for them on websites like Amazon or Half.com. I even found some books on Google Books for free. Often, the professor will tell the class on the first or second day which books we really need and by when we have to read them. In the meantime, many professors will hold their books on reserve in the library.*
>
> — Ashley Villanueva, University of California, Berkeley

▷ **Stock up on food and beverage staples in your dorm room.** If you tend to get hungry late at night or at hours when the dining hall is closed, always have some food in your dorm room so you aren't tempted to order takeout. Stock up on sandwich meat, bread, popcorn, trail mix, cereal, granola bars—whatever you like to snack on. And if you drink coffee, buy a coffee machine for your dorm room.

▷ **If you're older than twenty-one, limit your purchases of alcoholic beverages.** Those purchases add up. Instead of buying your own alcohol, go to fraternity or house parties that supply free beverages. If you must choose a bar as a location to meet up with friends, become a drink special aficionado. Almost all bars have drink specials on certain nights or times.

▷ **Attend school events and club meetings that serve free food.** College campuses are filled with these, so keep an eye out for when they happen—you may just get a free meal out of it!

▷ **Cut back on going out to bars and clubs, eating out, and ordering in.** It's to these activities that most of your money could easily go, so limit them to special occasions.

▷ **Use cash to pay for things.** It's easy to overspend when you can't actually see how much you're spending. Force yourself to budget by allowing yourself only a certain amount of cash to spend per weekend, for example, so you will have no choice but to use it wisely.

▷ **Don't buy groceries at the convenience stores on campus.** They may be convenient, but the prices are too high. Shop at a grocery store off campus, buy in bulk, and buy generic. Also, become a member of your local grocery store so you can get discounts.

▷ **Use your student discount!** Many stores and restaurants on and near college campuses offer student discounts. Often all you have to do is show your student ID card.

▷ **Walk or take public transportation whenever possible.** You'll save on gas.

Career Planning

"I'm just about to start college, and you're telling me I already have to start thinking about my career?" you wonder. Not so fast. I'm not suggesting that you map out a ten-year plan before you even begin your first semester. However, I am recommending that you start to take small steps toward knowing and building your skills and interests, learning about possible suitable occupations, and familiarizing yourself with job-hunting tools and skills.

Visit your college's career center. Most college students make the mistake of waiting until senior year when they are applying for their first job after college to visit the career center. Don't make this mistake. Pay a visit early on in your freshman year to get help with creating your résumé, learning interviewing skills, and applying for internships.

Create and maintain your résumé. Your résumé is basically a summary of who you are as a professional. It outlines your educational background, your skills and interests, and your employment history. You probably had to create a résumé when you applied for college or if you've applied for a job before. When you get to college, visit the career center and enlist a career counselor to help you write and edit your résumé, as well as to keep it up to date as you gain more skills and experiences. This document will become more and more important in your career: first when you apply for internships and then later when you enter the job market.

Learn interviewing skills. At the very least, being a good interviewee involves looking and acting professional, knowing the company and job you are applying for, asking the right questions, and articulating your strengths and weaknesses. Interviewing for internships and jobs is a skill in itself, and thankfully, your campus career center can help you learn how to interview well. Many even provide mock interview sessions.

Apply for internships. College is the perfect time to find out what type of career stimulates your interest. Internships provide an opportunity for students to acquire training in and knowledge about a particular field or industry, often in exchange for a small salary or stipend or for college credit. Make sure to apply for internships while you are in college. This is best done during the summer but can also be done during the school year if you have time. These opportunities are extremely valuable in skill- and résumé-building, as well as in building your career network.

Know the value of networking. Networking, which is making connections with other people for the purpose of creating career opportunities, seems intimidating, but it doesn't have to be. It's actually a lot simpler than it sounds. In college, all it involves is getting in touch with people who have knowledge about or work in a field you are interested in and asking them about what they do. Start developing relationships with your professors. Take advantage of their expertise, meet with them outside of class, and learn about how they got where they are now. Keep in touch with everyone you meet—even your classmates—because these connections could lead to job opportunities much later in life.

Conclusion: Looking back at four irreplaceable years

Every college girl's experience is unique, but we can also learn from each other, gaining and dispensing the wisdom that only experience can offer. No matter what happens, your four years of college are going to be irreplaceable, and you'll wish you could live them over and over again. Somehow it seems impossible to fit everything you want to do into just four years. You'll wish college were twice as long, just so you could have the chance to try everything.

Live life to the fullest while you're there—college is filled with opportunities that you may never have once you graduate. That's not to say life ends after college, but at no other time in your life will you get a chance to preview and sample every possible activity, personality, and relationship that exists in the real world.

The day you graduate, you want to reflect on these last four years without regret and with appreciation that you came away learning so much about yourself and the people around you. Every year of college will find you changing and always for the better. You'll grow as a person and as a woman. And with the start of each year, you'll look back on the previous one in awe of how much your attitude and perhaps even your view of the world has changed.

College is your preparation for the real world and not just intellectually. You learn the most, not from your professors, but from the people you meet and the experiences you have outside the classroom. Don't underestimate the value of the people around you. Get to know as many people as you can, and appreciate their idiosyncrasies and every story they have to tell.

Enjoy the uncertainty that characterizes college life, because after these four years, you'll have to make decisions and start moving in some sort of definitive direction. And while you're drifting, keep your eyes peeled for something you feel passionate about.

You'll know you've made the most of college if, in the end, you've changed for the better, made some great friends, and learned a thing or two about life. No matter what, have fun. Come to think of it, it may be difficult not to!